PICTURES, POEMS *and* PRAYERS FOR THE SOUL

Charles McCollough

Printed in the United States of America

GoToPublish LLC
1-888-337-1724
www.gotopublish.com
info@gotopublish.com

Also by Charles McCollough

The Morality of Power:
A Notebook on Christian Education for Social Change

Lifestyles of Faithfulness:
Resources for Outdoor Ministry (with Carol McCollough)

Heads of Heaven, Feet of Clay (illustrated)

To Love the Earth

Resolving Conflict with Justice and Peace (illustrated)

Faith Made Visible: Shaping the
Human Spirit in Sculpture and Word (illustrated)

The Art of Parables: Reinterpreting the Teaching Stories of Jesus in Word
and Sculpture (illustrated with CD)

The Non-Violent Radical: Seeing and Living the Wisdom of Jesus
(illustrated with CD)

Picture This: My Journey from Words to Images

CONTENTS

INTRODUCTION

This book has been a long time in coming. The pictures are of my drawings and sculptures created in my barn, and the poems are mostly made during my travels over many years. The prayers are from worship services I led at Barrington Congregational Church in Rhode Island.

My full-time occupation on the national staff of the United Church of Christ included travel throughout the world so there was a lot of time to write poems on planes and in airports. Only recently I thought of putting the pictures, poems, and prayers together. Some of the pictures of sculptures may look familiar to those who have seen some of my other nine books, but the pictures, poems, and prayers fit so well together that I put them together here. Also, since I'm right-brain dominant, I rarely miss a chance to visualize my thoughts and try to communicate both verbally and visually in words and in images. My hope is that readers/viewers of this book will give equal time to the images and to the words. Though some may have seen a few pictures of my sculptures or heard the prayers. I know no one has seen or heard the poems except my wife Carol McCollough and my friend and UCC pastor, Maren Tirabassi, who is a much- published poet and generous guide of my poetry. I accepted most all of her suggestions though she is not to blame for my wording.

As for Carol, none of the words or sculptures were possible without her patient encouragement and her wise suggestions of the college

English professor she has been. Most of the sculptures are terra cotta, fired clay. I have pieces in metal, stone, and wood, but the wooden ones are mostly of animals whose philosophy or theology is unknown. I have no poems for the wood, stone, or metal pieces. I am pleased that some bronzes have gone to famous heroes such as Nelson Mandela, Bishop Desmond Tutu, and Pete Seeger. Finally, I will present two examples of justice and peace making in Congress and in local churches. This book has three main sections and two stories in the Epilogue. First is a section about my early education. Then there are two chapters of poetry and prayers. The epilogue has two stories that are samples of my social justice work in Congress and one of my meetings in a church conference. Now I hope to share them for more to hear and see. I will start with a story of how I discovered that I think in pictures and images, as well as thinking in words and sentences and that I am dyslexic.

Figure 1: I have often thought I carried the world, if not on my shoulders, in my lap.

I grew up in a town we will call "Lower Branchwater, Texas" to protect the innocent and irritate the guilty. It was not much of a town back then; but in the years since I left, it's gone downhill from that. Lower Branchwater was the kind of place which if I talk about it much, even good, active listeners will doze off. It was mostly a cross road between Dallas and Ft. Worth, centered on the football field with an attached school house, two gas stations, three Baptist churches, and a few other buildings. That's all the buildings we needed to do all the things we had to do in Lower Branchwater, Texas. There was not much to do when it was not football season. You could break tar bubbles with your toes or go to one of the Baptist churches and praise the Lord.

We had two people who made it out of Lower Branchwater. One became nationally famous. He was Lee Harvey Oswald, who was accused of killing Pres. Kennedy. The other one was famous only to his immediate family... me. They carried Oswald out of town. I left of my own free will. My parents were great and very generous and deferential. Whenever I talked, they listened. My first word was to my Father: "Da, Da, Daddy?" He answered, "I don't know, boy; what do you think?"

Figure 2: Mama said, "Bend over, Son; you're gonna get it!"

Anything I wanted they got me. I thought my parents were great, but today they would be called 'permissive'. When I misbehaved my mother raised the belt to spank me and then thought a minute and said reflectively, "Since this is going to hurt me more than it hurts you, I think I'll just forget the whole thing." Not that I was spoiled from a spared rod, but I did like it when Mama guessed what I wanted for breakfast and served it to me in bed. That was easy: a big bag of Fritos and a Dr. Pepper.

Figure 3: I was a "good boy" in the family. My older brother had grabbed the "bad boy" role before I could get it.

My brother exercised the right of primogeniture. Freely translated by him, it meant as a big brother, if I had something he wanted, he would beat me up and take it. I would scream for help from my parents, but being permissive, they'd say, "Be patient, big brother is just expressing himself." It was not hard to get myself beat up back then because I was very small. I was so small they often counted me absent from school. I protested that I had perfect attendance. My homeroom teacher said, "No, there wasn't enough of you to count as 100% present." The teacher would say, "Everybody stand up for fire drill." Then she'd repeat it for me. "Charles, you stand up too." I'd answer, "I am standing up." I was the smallest person in all my classes until eighth grade. Then I passed up a little boy. He was in a wheelchair. But I did not catch up with girls until high school. At dances it was awful having to dance with the Amazon girls. I even got a black eye once when a really breasty girl made a quick turn.

With all these handicaps—small size, permissive parents, being pushed around by my brother—I had to decide what role to play in my family. I auditioned for the role of a whiney mama's boy specializing in temper tantrums to get my way. But I didn't get it. My brother again had already grabbed that role too. He was the star of the family. Uproar was his special scene.

So, I tried out for the family role of "good boy". It was easy. I had no competition this time. I played "good boy" very well. I was "good" in the worst sense of the word. I was obedient, disciplined, organized. . . rigid, obnoxious, and self-righteous. I was the perfect complement to my prodigal brother. Some boys were religious, but I did not take to it at all. I wasn't religious in the common meaning of the word "religious". But I was religiously devout in the real, functional religion of Lower Branchwater, Texas. That functional religion was, of course, works righteousness. Moral purity is rewarded and moral slackness punished. The most visible organization of the religion for boys was expressed in Texas football. There really wasn't any choice for boys. For girls, they could be cheerleaders or cheer-followers. A boy was either a football jock or a nerd. Like a Third World country, there wasn't any middle class. I decided to be a jock—but there was one problem. The only sports were basketball, which favored height, and football, which required weight; I was short and skinny.

Figure 4: I learned to run fast even though I was very small.

So, I did what I knew how to do–self-discipline. I would make myself bigger. I dieted, I exercised, and I prayed to get bigger—the things I do now to get smaller.

It slowly began to work a little. I gained ten pounds by my senior year. . . in college. On my high school football team, we had half-backs and quarter-backs. I was so small I played 7/16ths. But I compensated: I was fast. That wasn't natural either. Yet when a 225 lb. linebacker comes for blood after a 102-pound running back, he learns to move fast. I would jiggle around fast, get them off balance, then side step. That occasionally required me to run in the wrong direction when the only turf to jiggle around on was toward my side's goal post. This upset the coaches, so I warmed the bench a lot. So much, in fact, that the seat of my pants developed heat fatigue.

Also, I compensated by discovering my senior year that some sports, such as track and boxing, did not reward large size. You could be matched up in track and boxing with someone your own size. So, I took up boxing and ran high hurdles. I had other reasons to box. I was tired of getting beaten up by my brother and by an assortment of other bullies who just didn't like my face and wanted to move some things on it around. I trained hard. The big night of the Golden Gloves Tournament came.

I was to fight, of course, another light weight (maximum weight 135 lbs.). But one of those marvelous things happened that was new to me—my opponent was my own size. But still, I was scared to death. I had no excuse now. Then to top it off, he knelt down before the first bell rang and before his plan to batter me senseless and prayed for God to help him do it, crossing himself afterward with his gloved hand.

I asked my coach if that praying would help him win. My coach answered, "Not if he can't box." I got through it. According to the judges I lost, but for me, I won. I had survived. Like Rocky, I went the distance. I endured the punishment and took all he could give. I was still standing after the final bell. I went on to win the lightweight title the next year in Dallas and in Austin.

Figure 5: Boxing was great. I could fight little guys. . . my size. That's me landing a right hook.

MY RELIGION

I used to think I had no religion. Nothing could be more inaccurate. Sports was my functional religion. But there was also the public religion of the churches. I was a nominal church dropout. I'd call it now a "generic Methodist." Every Christmas and Easter morning I would roll over in bed with a twitch of guilt. . . and go back to sleep. Most people in Texas, however, are "atmospheric Baptists." Religion was in the air in Texas. You could not breathe without taking in a Baptist hymn, such as "Just a Closer Walk with Thee."

You could not see the hymn, but one would stick in your mind at breakfast and stay there 'til supper. I'd be running laps in football, humming, "Just a Closer Walk with Thee." It made you believe in spirits. You'd turn on the radio. There was Rev. Billy Don Sugg's Gospel Hour pumping the souls for cash. "Brothers and sisters in

Jesus, keep us on the air with your dimes and dollars." The Dallas Morning News did not have Nicholas Kristoff or Paul Krugman editorials. It had Billy Graham and Parson Prickett on the front page to keep morality in tow.

Some scholars claim that the Protestant religion has broken apart. Well, they forgot to tell the people in Texas. The magazines, newspapers, schools, and community all taught a moralistic religion of reward and punishment. If you're good, you will succeed in life. If you're bad, you'll end up living under a bridge.

With six days a week of this religion, by Sunday I was exhausted and ready for a Sabbath rest. So, I slept late.

Figure 6: I was drummed out of the Boy scouts by General Stout.

There wasn't much in Lower Branchwater, but as I said, we had enough churches. There were First Baptist, Second Baptist, Third Avenue Baptist, and Assembly of God churches. But the really high church for the upper class of the little town was a quaint, small red brick building with tall trees around it. That was the first and only Methodist church.

I attended it regularly for a period of time. Every week I went to a Boy Scouts meeting in the education wing until I was drummed out of the corps by Major General Seymore P. Stout, who court-martialed me for insubordination to the senior officer, Seymore P. Stout. While he lectured on tying a square knot, I was working on a merit badge in manual obscene sound-making in the back of the room.

I was not good all the time. That casual tie to the church, together with my parents' assumption that "Well, if 'anything happened' (code words for a death in the family), the Methodist church was where we'd go." These tied me like tape to being a nominal Methodist and seasonal flashes of worry about my absence from the church. I was not even very good at absence. Somehow the religion in the air taught me I should feel guilty.

Figure 7: I had a very casual tie to the church.

I did visit the Baptist church occasionally with friends and even the Assembly of God service with a girlfriend, but the effeminacy of the minister was an affront to my budding "jockismo". I was not attracted to ministers because they were not real jocks. It was easy to condemn religion in general and ministers in particular for their effeminacy. But somehow the steel trap logic of that theological justification did not hold for my girlfriend's church.

My girlfriend's church had an extremely effeminate pastor—a woman who also was her mother. Why fate had it that the most beautiful girl ever to walk the earth then had to have a mother who spoke in tongues, I'll never be able to explain. "Al hum wac yah ma." Maybe that meant "Bring her home on time or I'll see that you get zapped." You see, religion was everywhere.

While my nominal Methodism amounted to a limp safety net in case "something happened", the religion of self-righteous moralism took hold hard and fast. That is, good and bad behavior was the meaning and purpose for life and that is all there was to it. It defined my boundaries. A righteous judge and executioner was my god. It fitted very well my self-image of the good son, compared to my prodigal brother who arranged his life so that it seemed always to total up to chronic trouble: slammed doors, broken windows, wrecked cars, and flunked courses. He found his power in uproar; we all in the family cooperated as his stunned audience.

Figure 8: Her church had a woman pastor.

So, the role I played was "good boy." I would be good or else. What did it mean to be good? What was my real religion? In spite of my dishonorable discharge from the Boy Scouts, I was probably one of the most thoughtful, courteous, trust-worthy, kind, brave, clean, reverent Boy Scouts around. There were, of course, frequent lapses into badness as the powers of machismo, biology, and the real sins of arrogance and sloth and collusion had their way with me. But they were periodically corrected, and I got back on my road to goodness-brings-success and away from the prospect of a life of shame and disgrace living under the bridge with Billy Goat Gruff.

The movies on Saturday of Zorro, The Lone Ranger, and Tarzan undergirded my religion of morality very well. The untainted heroes provided the imagery and models of heroic purity that I was to follow: to right wrongs, to defend the helpless and turn my head away from temptations of aimlessness, wine and wild women. But the epitome of the hard work, moral purity, and religion was sports, especially football. It provided all the flagellation, physical sacrifice, and weekly ritual that any religion could offer. I was one of its most ardent devotees.

Not that I did not have fun in my childhood. I just did not enjoy it much. Fun, or too much of it, usually brought with it a lurking, haunting toll taker to collect a fee at the end. Whereas hard work, discipline, promise of future joy—never quite reached—but all-consuming in the reaching, ruled my spirit.

Like the institution of Boy Scouts, institutional religion defined as church was hardly a powerful force in my life. But I was good to a fault, religiously. I figured out a simple calculus. If the bad are punished with shame and misery and the good are rewarded with happiness and fun, I wanted to stick it out for the goodies. Why go to Calcutta when you can end up in Tickle City? But my ignorance of the Bible (where the rain falls on the just and the unjust and the hired hand who works less gets paid as much as those who work more) kept me in a simple world of good and bad throughout my childhood. So much so that sometimes when the guys were going out with evil intent, I was left at home with my boring goodness.

Figure 9: My brother was two years older and five years smarter than I was. He became an architectural engineer.

The big event that concluded a piece of my early childhood and dictated the way I would live my life for a long time to come (that is, which gods I would worship) happened when I was in senior high school. My brother continued to search for boundaries by having flunked out of or quit a few colleges and wrecked a few cars.

This situation made competition for our parents' car very intense. One evening I had plans to use it to take a date to a movie. He also had plans to take a date to a movie. A different date, a different movie... the same car. But I had the car keys. This required him to exercise (as a last resort, of course, if intimidation and threats did not work) his presumed right of primogeniture as he interpreted it: namely, to knock me down and to take the keys. Would he dare?

Now in the two years that he had been off flunking out of schools, he had chosen a life of waywardness and debauchery—he drank beer and smoked cigarettes. Meanwhile, I was in training, trying to be good and I'd learned how to box. I was disciplined. I got up at 6:00 a.m. and made lists. I worked out twice a day and went to bed early with a glass of milk. I was a one-man military academy. I also was a potential "Type A" heart attack victim at 17. At 18 I was ready for a mid-life crisis. I was a maximum achiever with minimum gifts. Then my brother made a strategic decision which turned out to be his mistake. He decided to exercise his right as the big brother with a "preemptive defensive strike", as the Pentagon might call it. He lunged at me with fists flying to get the keys.

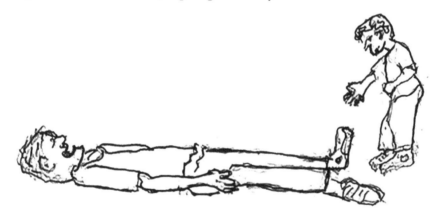

Figure 10: My big brother was not prepared for my skill of boxing.

When he woke up on the floor, we had a totally new relationship. The right of primogeniture ended that day in the living room of my parents' home. A lot of other things ended too.

I had learned that hard work pays off, that I did not have to be a victim all of my life and that a way to deal with the problems of permissiveness, smallness, and uproar is to be organized, disciplined, and tough. If I'd known what it was then, I'd probably have made a good right-wing Republican. But I knew nothing of politics. Nor did I have any idea about serious religion. I learned that day that certain tyrannies, like my brother's oppression, can be overcome by violent revolution. Or to put it more theologically, works righteousness worked for a while and that became my religion. It would be a few years before I learned that works righteousness would not save me, a few more years before I could name all these things that were going on in my life. But Jesus' story of seven demons replacing the one swept out, finally began to make sense to me. I didn't have to be a fatalist, a victim; life is not only a problem to endure stoically. Life, I came to believe, was a battle to be won against all odds, where good works righteousness will prevail over sloth and passivity even when the foe is bigger, older, and stronger. When the going gets tough, we wimps act tougher. "No guts, no glory" summed up the faith (what kept me going) as a kid.

Figure 11: Jesus got into fights too. He was held back from treating a demon-possessed man.

COLLEGE

After high school I went to a tiny college in North Texas which we will call The Elm Forks Baptist Academy, to protect the innocent and pious. I did not go because I was religious, let alone Baptist or because I liked a small school or that it offered an academic program I wanted. I went to this two-year college because it gave me an athletic scholarship of room, board and tuition if I could play football and other sports and sweep floors once a week in the dorm.

It could hardly be called a college by most standards. It was more like grades 13 and 14 of high school. In short, it was just what I needed.

Figure 12: The Elm Forks Baptist Academy

It sat on the flat Texas plains like four cactus plants in a vast level desert. It had as many old, red brick buildings: a gym, a classroom an administrative building with strange turrets and spires, and two plain, flat dorms three stories high—one for boys and one for girls. The treeless lawn was mostly Caliche rock. If the wind was not blowing, the dust was all over. It looked like the set for a haunted house film. I had to fight myself to go in the first time. I would have turned back if I had not come with a few high school friends to try out for the football team on a hot August afternoon. After a week the try-outers were cut to about 30 team members, and most of my friends got to go home. I was stuck in this desolate place because by some miracle or mistake, I had made the team. I could not figure out why, because although the other players were even bigger than those in high school, I still weighed only 128 lbs. My only explanation was that I was fast and a compulsive flagellanti. In reality, I was scared to death most of the time, but I hated the fear so much that I overcompensated with acts of evident but desperate boldness. A psychologist has called this counter-phobic. I think that theology once again helps explain what was happening better. I showed such boldness because I was so scared and I tried very hard to compensate. I tried so hard that a coach could hardly overlook me. The reason I tried so hard, I can see now, is the same reason that certain religiously fanatical soldiers can overcome soldiers twice their size. Winning in football was my religion. I was tiny but I would simply outwork, outrun, and be tougher than my competition. So, I made the team and was assigned the appropriate position of running back.

Figure 13: My football injury shipwrecked my life. My football religion died.

But you can only bend the laws of physics just so much with fanatical hard work. I was bound to get injured and I did. My bones and ligaments would bend only so much before breaking. During the first game, I received the ball and discovered in front of me a high wall of blue uniforms. My team, the Elm Fork Armadillos, as best as I can remember, wore yellow. I was hit by about five of the opponents all at once. And when we untangled, I could hardly see or walk. My left leg was bending the wrong way at my knee. I should have been carried off the field, but I wobbled off, defiant to the end. That ended my football career and my self-image as a famous player. The facts were clear: torn knee ligaments and cartilage, no more football, ever!

But the loss of my self-image stuck with me like a dead loved one. I simply could not believe that I was no longer a football player. It had been the temple of my religion of discipline and hard work. It was all I knew how to be. When the facts kept teaching me that over and over, I denied them, escaped them, got angry, bargained and only gradually accepted them. That injury was probably one of the best things that ever happened to me.

The school generously continued my scholarship, and by spring my knee had healed enough for me to run track and to box. I also worked for the school at odd jobs and was trainer and score-keeper for the basketball team. Yet for some reason I was lost. My god of wrath had failed me. Contrary to what I had come to believe in my early childhood, working hard and being good was not enough. It had not gotten me the object of my idolatry, football fame. So, I lived in a great limbo for months. I was angry. I had few friends. I hated the depressing, dreary little college. I hated most of my teachers and I hated almost everything.

Figure 14: An evangelist was brought in to convert the students.

Then in a cold, blustery mid-winter week, the Baptists strategically brought in an evangelist to warm up the religious zeal of the students. An evangelistic revival was held right on campus each year just when spirits were flagging. (This phenomenon may seem strange to people from other areas of the country, but as I said, religion is everywhere in Texas. Even state schools had "religious emphasis week" when religious speeches, if not revivals, were allowed.)

By this time my depression was at its worst, without football to define me or my god of hard work to assure me. As best I can figure it out, I really was ready to join the school, open my life to a new way, find friends and make the best of what felt to me to be a broken life.

So, when the altar call came at chapel, I was ready to join the other students who went forward to be with Jesus. I did not have the slightest idea what it meant to "accept Jesus as my personal Lord and Savior." But it did mean that something besides my own iron will-power was to have a chance to rule me at least for a while, and whatever this Jesus mystery was seemed to help me at that time.

I gave up my defiant anger. I tried to make friends and, to my great surprise, they responded positively. I gave my teachers a chance; I even said to myself "This school ain't Harvard, but it's all I deserve, and the teachers know a lot more than I do anyway." I started studying and being a "good boy" again. I set myself the goal of making good grades. Most of all, I gave up my old dead self. The football jock was no more. I not only needed this little school, I needed this Jesus, whoever He was, to get me a new life. When my proud self-image died, life opened up for me.

Figure 15: I needed this Jesus at least for a while.

I did not stay with Jesus very long in the sense that I had no interest in studying about Him or doing any of the usual church things. In fact, I could not stand those hymns and what I took to be the pious, effeminate ministers or the rigid do's and don'ts of the Baptist church. But my attitude about life changed drastically and the world seemed to be a happier place to live in. I believe a bit of grace entered by life in between the death of one of my childhood gods and the birth of a few more. I believe my childhood finally ended here and my adolescence began.

Sports did not die and I continued to run track and to box, but they did not consume me. There was now more room for study and friendships. Eventually these too became false gods that I would grow to worship, but first I would have to learn how to read and write and study. It was a brand-new world. I did not know it then, but studying also contained a terrible liability for me, like being small in football. I was dyslexic without knowing it. So, I inadvertently learned how to anticipate test questions, to outline the lesson, to condense and creatively store critical bits of information years before the computer programmers were doing it.

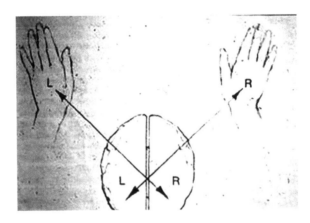

Figure 16: I was right-brain dominant, like my right hand and foot, so I preferred images to words.

My unknown disability made my world of school a crazy place. I remember reading only one book in high school. It was a library book on Kit Carson, full of pictures. Yet I had a B+ average and graduated in the top ten of my class of about 90 students at Lower Branchwater High. I would make horrible grades in math and on essay exams in class. But I made A's on true-false tests that required little reading. This disorienting experience of A's and F's, of extremes of ignorance and apparent intelligence, made the academic world seem like an amusement park. But I wasn't amused. I lived on a roller coaster never knowing if I would do well or bomb out completely. It was usually one or the other for a simple reason. I was good at everything but reading, writing, and arithmetic. That makes schooling difficult. Words and numbers seemed to move all over the page of a book, often reversing themselves. So "was" became like "saw." For example, "The magician approached the woman in the box, took out his was and wased her in half." The word "not" would sometimes jump to the next sentence.

Thus, a sentence that said "He did not like prunes, so he bought raisins", would read to me a "He liked prunes, so he did not buy raisins", which is gibberish—typical for me.

Figure 17: I drew lots of pictures to go with all the words in books that I read.

But given enough time and patience, I could go over the material sufficiently to figure it out. Even though I could barely read and write, I somehow thought I was not stupid. But I was not sure. My spelling was a joke because I perceived words to be spelled in a wide variety of ways. I had about three different ways to spell "choice." But I drew lots of pictures.

It took three times as long to finish study assignments and it was exhausting and discouraging. The world of books and words was just a wacko, crazy place for me then. What I see now is that what I did was to compensate verbally and visually. I drew pictures in class. Some of my class notes in college were drawings. I talked a lot, listened well, and took enormous lengths of time to prepare and read books at a snail's pace. I took speed courses and dumbfounded my instructors when I was still reading only a few words per minute after three such courses. I rewrote papers three or four times and tried to avoid having to read aloud to others at all costs. When I had to do so, people wondered if they were following me with the wrong book.

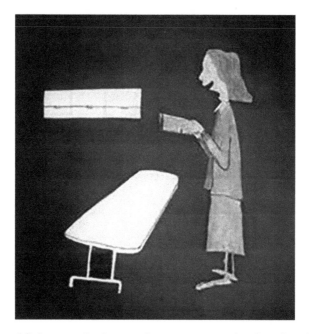

Figure 18: I was asked to read my essay out loud to the class.

The loony world I experienced was illustrated for me in a senior literature class. I wrote a paper on John Steinbeck's *Cannery Row*. Of course, it took me ages to do so. But the professor liked it so much that he gave me an "A". Then he ruined my fun. He asked me to read it out loud to the class right then and there. I could see my "A" melting into a "D" as I stumbled through reading the paper aloud before the class. I did not know enough about my problem to ask someone else to read it or to beg for time to practice reading it aloud. I did not discover what my problem was for about eight more years.

What possessed me to keep going to school so much after college was at least in part my religious fervor to be good, good at something. By my college years, "being good" had gradually expanded its meaning from moral purity and being a super jock to include good academic achievement as well. The in-class essays, math, and other deadly traps were less frequently inflicted on me in the social sciences, so I drifted toward that as a major. In this field term papers rather than classroom quizzes were used to measure my knowledge. I could plug along and make do when I had the time available for a term paper assignment. I remember the discouragement, however, when I watched a colleague take a stack of library books, speed read them, make notes on 3 x 5 cards on a typewriter, then sort them as if he were shuffling cards in a poker game. He would roll in a sheet of clean paper on his typewriter and type out his manuscript all in a day's work—ready to party in the evening. After watching this, I would look at the mess of books, notes, and false starts on my desk as one big puddle of finger painting. I missed a lot of parties.

The problem was that I was a handicapped person who had been mainstreamed without anyone's realizing it. I should have been held back as retarded years earlier (or even better, helped to overcome my disability). Instead, I got one big social promotion after another. School should have been a Special Olympics for me, but I was competing in the real world. I had learned in athletics that I could simply work harder to over compensate for my size. In college I did the same thing in my studies. I simply worked harder, outlining, making charts and pictures so I could understand a sociogram or a philosopher's thoughts. It took me so long to read a book that I usually had gotten very familiar with the author by the end of it. While my eyes were stuttering along trying to figure out all the confusion on a page I was reading, my mind was racing ahead to creating fanciful, wacko applications of the author's thought. If I could ever get the content off the page, through screwed up mental signals and into my brain, I never had any trouble making it relevant

I discovered later as a reader of exams for a history teacher at Brown University that many "A" students, the ones I hated and envied so much, could give back to the teacher all the content easily and fast, but it did not seem to make much difference to them. It was just one more "A" paper and a shot at another scholarship. By contrast, My "C+'s" and "B-'s" were bloody trophies of titanic battles with mysterious demons that constantly confused me so much that I sometimes thought I was going crazy. When I read about Martin Luther throwing his ink bottle at the devil once, for other reasons to be sure, I said, "Luther is my kind of guy."

But the excessive work required of me to keep up also had other negative side effects. I lived in a constant fear of someone reading my unedited papers, having to spell or read words that others would see or hear before I'd check them in a dictionary or memorize them. I remember trying to write a check to pay for some clothes once as the proprietor was watching me. I messed it up twice before I got all the numbers and letters arranged in their proper order. Usually I simply hid my torturous efforts at writing from public view. The result was that I felt like a fraud, a phony, a dunce in an intellectual world where I did not belong. For even if I could argue about Existentialism and talk about social theory, I was afraid that someone would spot my crazy spelling and take back my 8th grade certificate. And I had no defense, for it was true—I was a dunce in some things, but not in all. I knew and learned exactly what I heard in lectures and could outline it and feed it back easily, but reading in the textbooks was like adding some extra rocks for Sisyphus to carry up the mountain.

Figure 19: In college I looked for a mentor.

Since I had no name for my problem, the only explanations I had were my own laziness and inadequacy, which kept my self-esteem down to wimpish levels, and having attended a lousy school system, which kept my anger up to levels of divine wrath. I spent most of my early life embarrassed at my background, my schooling, and myself. But my cup of anger and defiance spilled over too and drove me on long binges of workaholism.

My student years were like those of many other students: a time to search for something heroic and important to be and to do. I did not know what it was. But I remember little else from that time than a desperate, unhappy search for a direction for my life and, of course, a director who could show me how to be and to do these heroic things. We now call it a "mentor." A mentor shows you how to respond to life; how to think, feel and act; how to get mad; how to be insulted; how to laugh; and how to gesture and eat spaghetti. I needed a mentor badly during my student years. I had had coaches to father and guide me in athletics and I kept them long after I phased out of sports to become a scholar. My coaches had showed me how to run, jump and hit, which was no help in a debate.

Figure 20: I moved in with my big brother at the university.

I looked around for mentors among my teachers, not realizing I was doing it. One English teacher, a middle-aged woman, helped me to open my eyes to poetry and to the horrors of racism through literature. But like the preachers, my female college teachers did not fit the macho self-image that I looked for.

When I moved on to the huge State University of Texas for my third year of college to live with my brother, who by now had settled down to study architecture, he was kind of a mentor; but I learned he was looking for a mentor also. I sought out teachers' responses to life I could try on for myself. Most were distant scholars who lectured to auditoriums of 300 or more students and disappeared behind body guards of graduate fellows. I did audit a philosophy course on Immanuel Kant taught by John Silber. He seemed to be mean and angry enough to fit my macho image of a man even if he only had one arm. He was famous on campus for his steel-trap logic and clever wit. But to think I could understand Kant enough at that stage (having taken only one philosophy course) to dare to ask a question in class was ludicrous. I dropped even this audit of his course before I flunked it. But I did not drop the search for a tough, macho mentor who could handle ideas and people intellectually the way my athletic coaches had whipped me and my teammates into shape physically.

Figure 21: I looked for a tough, macho mentor-an intellectual superman admired by all.

Then there appeared a challenger to the reigning monarch of rationalism, John Silber. This challenger was not another academic scholar like Silber. He was, of all things, a preacher. I could not believe a preacher existed who was not either sold out to the emotional gymnastics of revivalism or the prissy circuit of ladies' luncheons.

But the group of intellectual student leaders at Texas University, who by definition in the South were also interested in religion, at least during Religious Emphasis Week, were itching for a fight. Silber needed a challenger to curb the slashing logic with which he cut down even the best students. So, one night in the campus YMCA building, they set up a preacher who they thought was up to it, Joseph Matthews, who had been teaching in seminary but more recently had made the campus' speaking circuit throughout the South, establishing a reputation for flamboyant vulgarity, sharp, cutting humor, and convoluted displays of Kierkegaardian interpretations that few understood, but everyone enjoyed. He looked like a marine sergeant with a burly, stout frame and a gnarled face and moustache. His eyes were penetrating and his arms were always in motion with assertive, almost menacing gestures.

Figure 22: He offended everybody he could. We students loved it.

He was quite theatrical, but, above all, he was completely convinced and convincing in his beliefs. Stories were told of his offending ladies guilds by calling them all "whores--but for the grace of God." He called revivalist conversions "masturbating on a mountain top" and generally offended everybody he could. We students loved it. The debate was on some obscure theological point that I can't remember. Nor do I know who was supposed to have won it. All I remember is that the auditorium was packed full and many could not get in to see the famous John Silber either make mashed potatoes out of this preacher or see the preacher take on this supreme rationalist armed only with faith and wit. I understood little of what they said, but I do recall that the preacher Joe Matthew held his own, was very humorous, and gave me a drastically new image of what ministers could be. I had found a mentor. Matthews came to the University of Texas to teach at a resident community of students gathered under the title of Christian Faith and Life Community, founded by the Rev. Jack Lewis. By my senior year in college, I had replaced my athletic heroes with intellectual ones as my way of defining what I wanted to be in life. This community of about 80 men and women students was just what I needed to help me combine my search for a way to be somebody, a supportive community of disciplined study (two lectures and a seminar each week with theological reading assignments for each). The only thing that was difficult for me to connect was what this had to do with religion. It did not seem like the Baptist or Methodist churches I had known.

Gradually all the confusion of isolated specializations in my university study came together. By studying theology I found a reason for studying literature, geology, sociology and the other specialized subjects. The theological readings were an extra burden I could hardly bear, but the lectures and seminars were very helpful. I found a way to be myself in the world and it was, of all things, a religious way. I could not easily disassociate myself with all the negative images I had of the church. It had always seemed a weak, emotional appendage to life that I did not need; but here was an intelligent, rational kind of religion—a tough-minded faith that did not escape from the world. After a year and one-half of this religious community, I had finally decided what I would do with myself—go back to school after graduation and become a teacher of religion like my mentor.

Figure 23: By studying theology I found a reason to study literature, geology, sociology and other specialized subjects at the university.

Theologically, I now see my first conversion to be one of giving up a selfhood that had served me through late childhood—myself as a jock. My misery at not being able to play football drove me to anger and isolation that got so bad that anything looked better. The turning around directed me toward friends and an affirmation of my given place in a small college. I had no intellectual explanations of this, but it worked for me.

My second conversion was not away from the struggle but was an intellectual conversion in the world of confusing ideas and isolated compartments, all come together rationally.

The biblical miracles, myths, and language that had been claimed by irrational fundamentalism could also be claimed by existential liberalism. Seen in this light, they finally began to make sense to me. I said to myself: "If this is what Christianity means, I can believe it." Faith was no longer seen as believing what you know 'ain't so', but living authentically, open to the future and, as Matthews interpreted faith, 'living without defenses'.

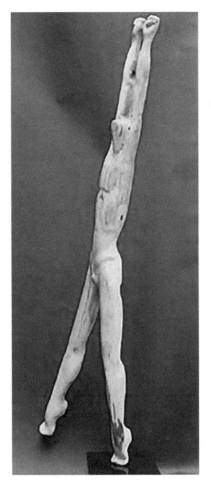

Figure 24: If this is Christianity, I can believe it.

I had so many defenses that my armor rattled when I walked. But it was a direction, an heroic goal that focused my energy. Faith and Reason could come together. Now after graduating from college, I was ready to begin my education. I found other teachers/mentors in Southern Methodist University's Perkins School of Theology like Fred Gealy, who taught me Greek and New Testament.

Figure 25: I found other teachers—mentors in seminary, such as Fred Gealy, who taught me Greek and New Testament.

EDUCATION BEGINS

Should the blind study painting? Should the deaf study music? Should the lame run the marathon? Of course not, but that's what I did! I set out for a Ph.D. in Theology because that is what I learned was necessary to become a religion teacher. I was blessed with the fact that I did not know at the time that it was impossible. Nor did I know, as I said, what dyslexia was.

However, in spite of the problem that I did not know I had, I did have a few things going for me. First of all, I was compulsive. It not only helps one in graduate study to be compulsive, it is a secret requirement that they don't tell you about in the graduate school catalogue. It's like the cranky, anti-social registrar or bursar who really runs the school but never gets into the public relations bulletins. Without them and the compulsives and masochists, you wouldn't have graduate school. There has to be a place for us compulsives. Graduate schools are out-patient clinics for us. Someone has to take care of us.

I looked compulsive. I wore horn-rimmed glasses, had six pencils in my shirt pocket and carried books. I had books all over me. I took books everywhere I went: on vacation, on dates, to bed. I was always afraid I'd get stranded somewhere without a book to read. I could not just sit down and enjoy life without a book. My bathroom began to look like the local library. I asked one of my professors of theology to give it to me straight, to be perfectly candid with me. What does it take to get a Ph.D.? He answered, "It's mostly having a hard ass." I was well suited in many respects to do graduate work.

Another thing I figured out to get me by was taking courses in the most obtuse philosopher and theologians available. Kierkegaard and Nietzsche had a way of narrowing the drastic distance between me and my colleagues. No one could read the guys fast and make much sense out of them. So, I would read Kierkegaard slowly and not make any sense of him either. That way it equalized the class. I began to feel that I was one of the guys.

Figure 26: Kierkegaard equalized us grad students. Few of us could understand him.

There were a lot of small techniques I picked up that I can recommend to other special, remedial students who happen to end up in graduate school. Since writing is difficult for us handicapped and mistakes occur every other word, I got to using huge erasers. In fact, those pencils I carried around in my shirt were really long erasers with a little piece of graphite stuck in the other end.

Figure 27: Nietzsche was a challenge to understand, but not only for me. His anti-religious philosophy challenged all of us budding theologians.

But the cleverest thing of all I did to get through graduate school was the easiest in a way. In fact, like most good things, you don't do them yourself. They just happen to you free of charge. It's called Grace. A couple of years after college, I fell in love. Now, I know that love could be a terrible intrusion into serious academic pursuits. It could have been, indeed, but I didn't just fall in love with a beautiful young woman who was smart, talented, fun, and rich. I fell in love with such a woman who also was an English teacher. For some reason that is still a mystery of grace to me, she reciprocated my love and became my editor-in-residence. Without her I'd still be stumbling through Kierkegaard's *Either/Or*, lost.

I also got a break financially by getting a tuition scholarship to a three-year prep school for theological graduate students. Some called it seminary, but it was a way for me to start getting an education for the big leagues. I was going for a Ph.D. or else!

So, with my wife's help and my own compulsiveness, I muddled through more years and years of study. The biggest agony for me was foreign languages. I <u>had</u> to know French and German, and I had better get Greek and Hebrew. Also I added Spanish as well because a Spanish philosopher was to be the subject of my dissertation. But I was not great at English yet. I got another "social promotion" in Greek and forgot about even trying Hebrew. Then I set out to learn Theological German for about three years. Theological German is a lost dialect of Hoch Deutsch. It's a wild old Teutonic game in which you open a fat book of tiny print with few periods and a voice says to you, "I dare you to find the verb on this page, *Dumkoff!*"

Figure 28: Besides her musical talent, Carol was also an English teacher. She got me through.

My learning problem was not much worse in German, French, and Spanish. I went about as fast in Greek as anyone else in class.

We all read it one sentence per hour. "In-the- beginning-God...."
But I took the German exam four times. When a visiting German
professor read my attempt at translating, he went off in a Hitlerian-
type tirade.

One crazy attempt I made was translating a book from German
called *Wehrheit und Methode*, by Hans Georg Gadamer. It seemed
important at the time. So, I went to it looking for the verb and
looking up every other noun as usual. However, something was
different this time. It began to make perfect sense to me. I was
on drugs and it read like a story book. I had a bad cold and had
saturated myself with some potent anti-histamines. For once in my
life I could read easily—and in German—theological german at that.
The drug wore off, however, and I returned to plodding along. But it
was a really ecstatic, mountain-top experience for a theological nerd
alone with his books. Had I been in medicine or alchemy, I might
have tried to figure out what happened, set up a language school,
feed students Dristan, and run Berlitz out of business; but that's
another lifetime.

Figure 29: Trying to translate theological German

What, you may ask, does all this theology have to do with religious
faith? Now I believe that one <u>can</u> go through graduate school of
theology and remain religious. I also believe in the tooth fairy. In one
sense it has very little to do with faith. Scholarly study of religion
and the teaching of it may be as mundane as yesterday's newspaper

or competitive as a pool of sharks. In fact, the theological debates between various schools and factions often got so rowdy that helmets and shin guards should have been recommended.

It was a deep exercise of faith. It was a sincere act of devotion to god. The only problem is the god was the god of the wrong religion. It was not the God of Christianity but several versions of the god of Gnosticism. The ultimate value I got caught up in was a god of knowledge. To know correctly is to be saved. This, of course, was not what was taught, and each student and teacher had their own devotional life that I cannot judge; but for me what really counted was knowledge over faith, reason over conviction, and grades over goodness. After years of research and learning how to write so that no one could understand what I was saying, I was tempted to assume and behave as though my entire existence depended on passing the next course or finishing the dissertation.

I started writing my dissertation eventually because my wife informed me one day that I had nine pregnant months to finish it and get out of the library and into a legitimate paying job. So, it became a kind of race between her childbearing and my book learning. Well, it wasn't even close. She won the race by two years and had our son about a year before I sent in the first draft of my dissertation, which I was sure would jar loose a few tusks of ivory from the tower once it hit the newsprint on the lecture circuit. Sending my manuscript off to my professors was a great relief. Getting it back was the problem. By this time my whole being hinged on passing and getting that degree that I had come to worship with all my heart, soul, mind, and strength. And I assumed that the whole world expected it of me. I should have graduated two or three years ago. Of course my wife expected it. I was 30 years old before finding a real job. I even thought in my absurd, idolatrous way that our one-year-old son also demanded it of me. So, there was no way out. It was either pass and graduate or dispose of myself in Samurai fashion as the only other honorable expiation of the disgrace of failure. Gnostic gods don't mess around. The package arrived in the mail. I brought in the envelope containing the word of my fate. I opened the package. It was bad, really bad. I did <u>not pass</u> and I was told that if my dissertation did not undergo radical surgery, meaning start over and survive the committee, I was doomed. I wanted to die. I had been at this for ten years since college. I had no energy left for it. A dark shroud of gloom descended on me. I think it was raining. I sank down at the kitchen table in total despair and began deciding which weapon to use.

Figure 30: I was doomed when my dissertation was rejected.

Then my son waddled in. I did not want him to see me like this. I turned my head away in dejection. He was quiet for a change. I thought he had left. But after a while I felt something being put into my drooping hand. It was wet, slimy and round. He had put a ping pong ball from his mouth into my hand, his gift of healing spittle.

I turned to face his jeering hostility over my shameful performance. But he just smiled up at me and reached out for a hug. For some reason he accepted me—even without a Ph.D.

That was my third conversion. This time it was from Gnosticism back to the grace of God freely given—made of flesh—from a child.

Figure 31: I was called to a local church.

My cup of grace began to overflow then when I got the Ph.D. back into focus as something no one required of me but myself. And it had nothing to do with my salvation or damnation, at least not in the Christian religion that I professed. My second gift of grace was that doors to college teaching had closed for me, and a call to a local church to be a teaching minister had opened. I took two weeks off from my church job and finished the revision of the dissertation with my wife editing as she retyped it (with four carbons, before the day of the personal computer). I passed the oral defense easily enough since I never had much trouble verbally communicating. As I left the final two-hour grilling by the graduate faculty, a colleague and his wife met me to hear the news. He was in his tenth year of the grad school grind with two children. They had come to celebrate with me, but I noticed they had brought a stretcher just in case. When I told them I'd passed, the wife said mockingly to her husband, "If Charles can do it <u>anybody</u> can!" No better putdown and no truer words could have summed up that moment of grace and glory.

Only a few months later, more grace and irony came to me. I read an article in *Time Magazine* about a new theory of a learning disability. The description of the symptoms fit me perfectly, but I did not dare believe the list of geniuses who the article claimed had the malady.

The most widely held theory was that this disability is caused by a poor or mixed signal system between the right and left sides of the brain. The result is an inability to perceive written symbols properly. One theory called it "stuttering of the eyes", resulting from a mixed dominance where neither the right or the left side can take charge. A lot of wild things happen as a result: ambidexterity, constant reversals of signals, horrible spelling, and an occasionally good artistic expression since the right brain, with its special capabilities for imagery, often compensates for the literal blunders of the left side.

Figure 32: The Dyslexic Advantage by Brock L. Eide, M.A., and Fernette F. Eide, M.D.

I found a school that was testing and studying the learning disabilities. Ironically, it happened to be in Texas, so I went there on our next visit to see our parents. I took the simple test which confirmed the fact that I was indeed quite learning disabled. I had "dyslexia" and learned that while I was right handed and right footed, my right-eye view dominated my left eye view. When the man testing me asked what I did, I told him I had just finished getting a Ph.D., he did a double take and said, "Sure, and I'm into space travel as a hobby. You're kidding of course." I said I wasn't kidding but that I had found it rather difficult. He still did not seem to believe me, but as I left he suggested that I return for more study. I believe he wanted me as a test case of something. But I left not really believing what I had heard. I thought it was only a theory; besides there seemed to be no easy cure, no drug or quick fix I could get.

Figure 33:" Ph.D.! You've got to be kidding, of course!"

All the studies that I read subsequently said that the only help was remediation—a nice word for "go back and learn it all over again," which I already had spent a huge chunk of my life doing. Indeed, I had gradually over about 20 years improved enough to manage pretty well. I learned to sound out words slowly and improved my spelling by grinding repetition. But the grace-full news to me was that I was not alone in the prison of demonic pranksters who moved letters, words and numbers around to trick me. These little monsters did not exist except in some twisted wires in my head; and by now at 30 years of age, I had traced out many compensating detours around these wires so that I could not only cope in the world, I could begin to minister to others who had their own demons to contend with. I found myself to be a good listener to others because I had been blessed—I called it "blessed" in my moments of faith at least—with these detours and obstacles to cope with. I know the loneliness of being different, but I've come to see that being different is just the point. We are <u>supposed</u> to be different, unique--out of chaos—a work of art, that is, never a copy but always made without a pattern. God does not paint us from numbers, and God seems to keep insisting that we be the most unique us we can be. In those moments that I have been forced to be me, all upfront, raw and vulnerable, I have felt also those rare moments of grace. And your acceptance of this story could be one of those moments.

Figure 34: Maybe we were supposed to be different. Jesus certainly was.

Now I will present some poems with drawings. They get to a deeper level of the spirit than the previous essay.

POEMS

LIST OF POEMS

- Art Show Opening
- Daughter
- Hurricane
- Child
- The Wall
- Hot Hazy Humid
- When the Pastor Calls
- Dream
- Geese
- Teen Girls in September
- Maybe the Time Will Come
- When Death Comes
- Why Don't You Call?
- It All Seemed Hopeless
- Which Me Will I Be?
- If We Could Be
- On Being You
- Where Did My Childhood Go?
- And We Both Cried Her Loss
- Tired
- Down
- Son
- Cold on the Trail
- The Moon Last Night
- The Storm
- Rain
- Morning Fog
- To Let Loose Some Joy
- When Stopping for Vacation

- Family Reunion
- The Old Fighter
- Vacation for Workaholics
- Sleep
- When They Finally Leave, the Children So Quickly
- Zealot's Fair
- First Grandson, Dylan
- Blossoms
- The Dreamers
- Hurricane
- Work
- The Child in Me
- Dead-Beaten Dad
- These Wounded Heroes
- At Ponca Creek
- Standing Rock Reservation
- Fort Berthold
- Home Now
- Zero Tolerance
- Fireflies
- Gene by the Sea

ART SHOW OPENING

Almost lost in the readying
anxious cleaning
repairing, and preparing
was the point of the show:
to invite others to a
birthplace party.
A room of spirit emanations
made visible and presentable
and even maybe marketable
after the bloody and raw
mess of creation.
Who would come to a real birth?
The tickets would rot.
But who does not seek
the life force that brings
us back to a rebirth
of our own souls?
That coming-from-spirit
to touchable, seeable form
is a magic we seek
in sometimes sick and silly
symbols and symptoms
and even teeter with
money, value, worth,
sales and purchases
to buy and vend the magic of life.
Who would dare price it?
But who would dare not sell all
to buy that treasure,
whatever its mystic measure?
That's the game and goal
near lost in the chatter,
food, drink
and surging small talk,

dipping and careening
in the crowd up and down
the topics of technique to
meaning to "How are the kids?"
Am I host or vendor,
guru or friend-er?
Am I valet, domestic,
artist, defender
of these births of art?
Mothered by muses
or demonic fuses
of countless containments
mere student arrangements
much searching unknowings
wanderings through wild
channels of escape, need,
love, anger and outrage,
these works of creation
come like a garden's goodness
and weeds-imitating fruit,
some of which we seed
and nurture only.
The opening and the show,
the creation and the birth,
we neither do nor know.

DAUGHTER

Off you go again. . .
now to Vermont.
But not Vermont so much as
Vermonters who've got to be
worth all the packing, better
than real life Jerseyans
and worthy of making you
worthier
and healthier and
hopefuller of becoming a better you.
I see no reason not to dream
such a dream into reality
if to stay awake in Jersey
is to wish for a different you.
Just because your father affirms
the present one does not mean
you can even stand another Jersey
minute of her.
So, if the dream pulls you north
to such a betterment,
my missing you has to step aside
for more of you to miss,
and the better you find yourself,
the less of you in me
I will have to mourn losing.
Call. . . collect!
Dad

HURRICANE

A hurricane levels homes
as if they were confetti,
and a storm of lies clutters
grim city streets
as politicians meet
to twist truth beyond bother.
Then we gather our tools
to search out the roads
that define us
and build again
paper homes
that hope to shelter
brief moments of truth
and small spaces of trust.

CHILD

There are the children, of course,
so evidently growing
far beyond my reach.
But there is also the child
in me who is so close,
I can't see him.
But he rages around
inside me at other's offenses,
purrs with satisfaction
at my indulgences,
and turns cartwheels at rare enchantments
that I, the cautious parent,
push so far away
that my orphan may,
with his silent outrages,
break me in
to let him out.

THE WALL

The wall is you inside:
broken, shattered by other forces
you don't affect—
just a barricade for armored courses.
Shelter, love, and care—now so far,
they can only mock the streets of war.
One hand shields from yet more pain.
The other supports you from death's reign.
Will the wall be your only brace
till your feet can
free those hands to grace
some small world of peace?

HOT HAZY HUMID

I gave it a hard, heavy, heated try.
That is all the effort I could heave
into the steamy, sultry, sweaty, sizzling
sauna summer.
It was just what I'd dreaded
even more so,
as my shirt settled solidly glued to me,
my pants filled up
wetter than a diaper,
and my head poured out fluids
surely essential for mental stability.
For little was left when
I clawed my way into a big piece of
ice in the freezer
and sat there
throwing talcum powder
on the coils
to hear the ice crack
and to test the machine's strength
against this human kiln.
Sure enough, it failed the test
and melted down into a chain reaction,
and citizens for miles around
were evacuated
and had to stay in school houses in Hudson Bay
till a blizzard from the North Pole blew
an all-clear signal.

WHEN THE PASTOR CALLS

Why does the house have to be so clean
as if our sins are seen
on the dirty dishes,
blasphemy felt on crunchy floors,
or heresy found on cobwebbed doors
when the pastor calls?
It's because he is supposed to be
what we suppose he's supposed to be,
I suppose.
And because we are so far from what
we're supposed to be,
it rarely occurs to us to ask if he is
what he really is supposed to be
when the pastor calls.
Which gives him the aura of the
Right Reverend Supposed-To-Be,
whose heavenly goal,
 by scientific count,
causes parish homes to be
15% more earthy
and 12% less worthy
of what he's supposed to be.

But suppose the Right Reverend
could be wrong
or at least tainted
by earthly commerce by even 1%.
Then since he ain't what he's
supposed to be,
he must be worse
than anything allowed in our
spic and span houses,
which after all are,
next to cleanliness, godly havens
they are supposed to be.
For if there is anything worse
than a falling angel,
it is a calling devil.
No sir, we gotta draw the line somewhere
when the pastor calls.

DREAM

I dreamed I woke up
but couldn't get up
because I was asleep.
And I couldn't go back to sleep
because I already was.
But that didn't stop
my dream from slapping me with wet towels
at my ears,
for it had some urgent primal
problem to solve.
And all I wanted to do was sleep.
So, I suggested a compromise
to solve the problem by just
dreaming I was asleep.
It agreed, though begrudgingly,
because this problem wasn't primal.
But even that solution would not matter now
because at last this terrible dream
woke me up.

GEESE

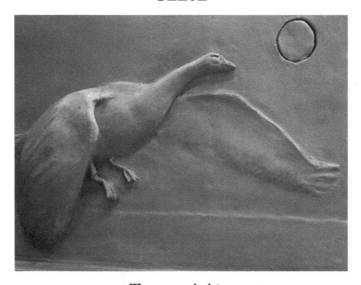

The geese babies
marching in line
between geese parents
last spring
have suddenly grown
out of line
this short summer.
And I missed the miracle:
waddling fuzz troops,
now discharged to an
adult beauty of
honking calls and
the pure grace of
landing glides.
They will soon
lead their own
columns of new life
for which I got
season tickets.

TEEN GIRLS IN SEPTEMBER

School,
new sharp pencils and erasers with edges,
cool breezes, painted trees, apples,
football, soccer,
canning, freezing, and storing
and piling wood.
But also
fear of failing and misunderstanding
too many assignments poured out too fast
for my slow brain to absorb
because the teachers don't know
it's already full up
and demanding more attention
from other subjects such as:
new GIRLS with every mysterious wonder

of their difference and
girls with new skirts swishing past
my longing—
fearful of even slipping across
the hazy caste lines
with treacherous enforcements,
and finally girls,
most pretty, and others like my cousins,
ordinary and just as traumatized as me,
some more so, I now see
because they must run the gauntlet of BOYS,
which, I guess, I would not trade
my fear for.
But that's hindsight, not now-sight,
for back then September was doom and gloom and
dread-full anticipation of too much glut
of failing assignments to be canned and stored in a
hot kitchen already brewing intoxicating
harvests of dangerous, undefined infatuations.
Can there be any more room to pile in the new harvest,
or can some of it wait for the eleven other months
and a lifetime to learn not to have to store it in
all at once?

MAYBE THE TIME WILL COME

Maybe the time will come
when I don't need from
outside what it can't give
to make me really live.
For I yearn to fill the old
aching gaps that mold
my damaged soul
where memories prey upon my nows
and explode at mere reminders
of past thens
like time bombs from ancient wars
fought for nought.
Maybe the time will come
when the past ceases lurking
and, like time capsules, starts sparking
my present with fireworks of fun
and bubbling joys of child enchantments.
Maybe that time will come
and I will be a brass band
welcoming committee marching
down Main Street in full
dress regalia
when the time comes.

WHEN DEATH COMES

Death, where is your sting?
You are our long partner on this short journey.
You shadow us in our days and frighten us
through our nights.
You come near in sickness and war and
whisk by with close calls.
You reach into our hearts and pound them hard
when you take away ones loved.
But we have other friends on this journey longer still
who salve your sting
and spoil your victory,
who mend our broken hearts
and break your fearful spell.
Death, you don't load us down long,
for we have loving friends
to carry the weight of sorrow.
We have Jesus' eternal promise to wash away our doubts.
we have memories of love, moments that lift us
over your hellish pain and join us to
God's timeless reign.

WHY DON'T YOU CALL?

Why don't you call
and destroy the pall
of horrible flashes—
wrecks, death and crashes?
In silence I wait
for your ring to abate
for chatty reports of mundane things
my relief from disaster brings.
Of course, you know that all is right,
thinking not of my doomed fright,
 assuming I by your sight see
and sit content to let you be.
But I can't see from your pure view
nor look upon your day anew.
I rather incline toward dread to find
Some grave catastrophe to mine.
Maybe it's time to sing
of what my day will bring—
enough of worry, fuss and rhyme,
sure to occupy my time.
But if doom does sound,
fretful props can't ground
my wildest shame at sights so few
and past moments lost from you.

IT ALL SEEMED HOPELESS

Then God's angel
through a gray-haired saint
woke me up and
said "No, it ain't
ever hopeless.
You have to stop."
"What!" I screamed.
"I tried it all;
don't tempt me with hope.
We're destined to fall."
It all seemed hopeless,
and so it was.
We danced the dance of death
like a demon does.
"All but one," she said,
"one you can't see.
Your hope is dead;
it need not be."
"Stop your hopeless tune,
for without your fated sound
the dance will stop soon,
'til a new tune is found."
I dared to hope
and so it was
we started to live
like a new-born does.

WHICH ME WILL I BE

Which me shall I be today?
Say, the careful one
ready for a ton
of toxic tongues?
Or Mr. Loose Goose
ready for
nothing taller than I can
man?
If better comes
to worse,
I could only nurse
a verse
or two
or tighten up
Mr. Loose
to a careful knot
so that tongues tied
to trailers
of noxious fumes
bounce free
and don't stick on me—
nowhere, never, nothing.
But then worse can't become
better, the vulnerable goose
with wounded tush.

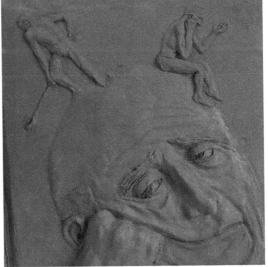

IF WE COULD BE

Free to fall
naturally
to the just right
me for each case,
we'd have a base
of reality unwobbled
and could, unhobbled,
solve this world's
problems in no time flat,
flattering ourselves with the
certitude that
a soft me only
meets a soft you
and hard waits
for hard times.
But just right is
still a long way off
and now hard me's
blast soft you's.
and soft you's smother hard me's.
But we're evolved
at least enough to see
how nice
if we could be
free to fall naturally.

ON BEING YOU

Of course, I want you to be you.
However miserable you may be,
it's at least predictable,
and I can go on assuming
you'll be you
and so I'll be me too,
unless you become you #2
in which case I'll have to
make adjustments and
contingency plans #1 and #2.
But if you become #3,
I'll have to build in an
escape route as me #3,
so that you #4
will not total me,
being as I my selves are
a total of at least four me's
predictably.

WHERE DID MY CHILDHOOD GO?

It feels like
they gave away my childhood,
of course, without intent, plan or desire.
But it's gone now
like the frolicking kitten,
lost down in this
crabby old cat – GONE.
Theirs was taken away with their
parents' early deaths
so that it seems they expected
a parent of me to see
firm care and gentle strength and
all the other impossible paradoxes
of parenthood putting painful pressure

on me that might free
them from their child's adulthood.
"What do we do with your naughty brother?", they asked,
as if I had a clue or a few things to do
about his wild cries for taming.
Having none did not stop me
from getting so yoked that I must still
stifle the rage
at that adult job
assigned to this powerless child,
not yet trusting that
I don't have to be a weak old cat now,
any more than
I had to be a strong young kitten then.
Can this tough, aging tom
still frolic again?
Only if for me the dead can die
and the alive can live.

AND WE BOTH CRIED HER LOSS

And we both cried her loss.
Yet I, a close but distant friend,
gone today and here tomorrow,
could only hope to ever mend
a tiny fragment of his sorrow.
We both fought the flow of tears
as moments felt like passing years
of loss like crushing ocean waves
gouging out a cliff of caves.
"She sat in that, her special chair."
"She shivered in the evening air."
The mornings here were always best."
Confirming thus their common quest
of day's routines, denying deaths,
securing them their numbered breaths.
And we both cried her loss.
Reports of other mourners' pain
seemed to lift the dark again
for lightening seconds of relief
from night storms of swollen grief.
Their children also hurt and fell
deep into that aching hell

of the endless cosmic quiet,
but she was with us all around
in ways unclear but too profound
for us to shake or long ignore,
bidding us to fly and soar
to far beyond our common sense
while we tried on the passing tense.

And those moments that we flew free
tasted for us eternity.
Again the tears began to flow
whenever we would start to go
back from Spirit's freeing hold,
back into our daily mold.

His tears were many and quick to see,
but mine were less and yet to be.
His tears were for the sudden past
and for thoughts that always shock,
but mine were for a saddened now
awaiting hence my future knock.
And we both cried her loss,
a new and motherless scary night.
And we both cried her loss.

TIRED

Can't run, can't walk
Can't jump, can't talk
Can't buy, can't sell
Didn't notice when I fell
Can't work, can't think
Can't smile, can't wink
Can't hear, can't see
Wonder if I still can pee
Can't stand, can't sit
Can't more, can't get
Braced to take another hit
Wrung out, beat down
Got home, bed found
Now so tired
can't lie down

DOWN

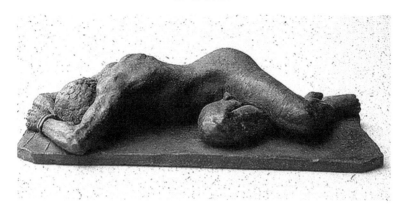

Down on the bottom
it looks so grim;
down in the darkness
the lights are dim.
You sink to sad center
that retreats from the hold.
You crawl into yourself
shaping a fold.
Down there's not wrong.
We need it to stay
sane in a world
crazier each day.
But finally you'll move
out from this rest;
the time will come
to forfeit your nest.
To another who's
downed by sanity's claim
you'll give up your cave
so compassion can name
your own center that's
lost now in its gain
when others replace
your self with their pain.

SON

Your eyes take in a world I do not know
from a book I cannot read.
Your long fingers grasp that world
and hold it firm.
Let me in for a moment to see
is it terror or ecstasy?
Is it a drugged escape because this
beyond the book is so sad?
Can there ever be such a glance at all or
are you now shut away in your world?
Please, if I can't come in,
will you glance out so I can
touch your soul again?
I weep to think that you are gone
from me even as you stand
long and intent
lost in a child's world afraid to come
to meet me as another man.

COLD ON THE TRAIL

Walking an old trail
will usually fail
to open my eyes
to any surprise.
Bent toward my aim
stooping my frame,
I lock in my gears,
harness my fears,
close up my ears,
restrain my tears.
I fold in my nose,
keep mouth closed.
Nothing can stay
my determined way
to stop disarray
of this planned day
except maybe a stop
when a bird would drop
a mess of a plop
right on my head.
With my plans dead,
I have a new chance
to awake in a glance,
emerge from my shell,
hot on the trail,
heaven-bent from hell.

THE MOON LAST NIGHT

The moon last night was
as large and close as it will
ever be,
as long as I will
ever be
here, at least.
And a simmering oak log
was sending out
just enough smoke
to scent the air with delight
and around my dull, busy
brain with word that
this moment was eternal.
And the old fishing boat
did not even try to hide
the moonlight,
but rather, enhanced its glow.
So, I had to know
that this moment of splendor
had to be a perfect enchantment,
but also dangerous beyond admission.
So, I retreated to the evening news
for which my caution had already
bought tickets.
But tonight when God sent
the geese honking on a gliding landing
across the moon sight,
I risked the devastation
of ecstasy.

THE STORM

The wind bullies the trees,
smashes loose things down
and loosens stashed things up
in a ravishing righteous way.
Snow sheets blast
like crazed white insects
my windows
blowing down
to rolling dunes.
Clattering ice pellets the roof
and jet streams of cold air
betray unknown
cracks in my walls.
Like my cold ventures
into unknown worlds,
the danger chill factor
freezes my easy way
to rigid controlled steps
and cautious moves
to assure my footing
in the fearful world.
But now I sit secure
near a wood stove,
warm and safe
inside an inner warmth,
knowing that this storm
will also pass
and, where streaks
of grace allow,
the warm shoots
of hope will
open my path
to safe havens
in other storms.

RAIN

Sure, we need the rain;
it washes us anew.
But now's a soggy pain.
It's overdone its due.
It hangs around and flows.
Its dampness oozes down.
It gushes as it goes
sloshing through my town.
It drizzles and it spits.
It dribbles and it splashes.
It leaks in all the cracks and slits
and washes through my lashes.

Rain's not just wetness from the sky,
nor lots of H_2O's.
It gets inside your psyche by
seeping through your toes.
It gets into your chest
and starts your sniff and sneeze.
It gets in all the rest
to bring you to your knees.
Working in the brain
it starts to drive you nuts.
You'd surely go insane
by now if you had the guts.
You have become a loon.
Your will's a soggy dish.
You'd rant and rave to Neptune,
but you've only evolved into a fish.

MORNING FOG

Whatever it's called by the weather predictors,
morning fog sets into the soul,
reduces the world
to a few feet
and expands the ghost's reign
a thousand miles.
It reminds me of
how little I know and
how much I pretend
each bright and sunny day
is manageable.
Breathing
the ghost's fog deep inside me,
I manage a few easy routines
and fake the rest,
I guess,
because a few others
in the fog's reign
are just as lost or more.
Now the sun begins
to whiten my page
and push more trees
and lighted cars into sight.
And I begin to miss the cocoon
of un-pretension.

TO LET LOOSE SOME JOY

To let loose some joy,
a wild and reckless whim,
it's too close to toy
with the fallen angel's hymn.
With fetters gone and routine
wrecked, we tempt our tattered plans
to stage a revolution scene
and march on shifting sands.
To drums of chaos' roar
we risk a joyous view.
We'd let emotions pour
as if it was safe to do.
But either/or's the way.
Joy will break the cast
where usual business's sway
is overrun at last.
Joy is decorum's doom,
so caution is our guide.
But given just the slightest room,
joy takes us for a ride.

WHEN STOPPING FOR VACATION

When stopping for vacation to rest
the routines and the plans,
I've seismic shifts within my chest,
volcanos in my glands.
I can't sit down
or stand upright
or go to town
or hold in sight
one clear task
or focused chore.
I jump and gasp
and look for more.
I fiddle here
and fizzle there.
I wander near
and change my wear.
I start at this

and jump at that.
Calls I miss.
I'm getting fat.
I rush upstairs
for one clear aim;
then back downstairs.
It's all the same.
Forgot my way,
lost my time.
Clocks don't obey.
Lines won't rhyme.
"Freedom" they sell.
I'm not so sure.
Kierkegaard's will
keeps the heart pure.

FAMILY REUNION

The dream of a family reunited
is the most durable dream
and the greatest awakening.
All together in the mind
they smile and hug
and pitch into the joyous
festivities.
There, in hope, is no pettiness
or peevishness, parsimonious pickiness.
no feelings set out
bait-like to be hurt,
justifying pouts and
proving favoritism or whatever
else needs proving.
In the dream there are
no overworked Martha's
begrudging Mary's

hair-drying, time-wasting,
show-stopping non-productivity,
no late arriving early-leavers
nor early-arriving-late leavers.
no spilt milk, just as the
store closes for the duration.
no dreary weather locking
us together after small
talk ended,
and large talk is all
that dangerously remains.
The dreams of a family reunited
has this and
all else that can go wrong,
and did,
locked out so that we
at least not for the dreamers

who never lack the
dream induced energy
to keep on arranging
the next perfect reunion.
And, lacking the dream,
all others are too tired to stop them.
So somewhere between the dream
and the waking uproar must
be life forcing past the
deadening done deals and,
holding fate at bay long
enough to let dreams,
at least in part,
come true.

THE OLD FIGHTER

Was there ever a choice
not to fight?
I can't recall.
Though it might
have been in the distant past
so far back it's lost,
for I made my bed
before I priced the cost.
Only "to battle"
that drum would beat.
I had to win
or die in defeat.
Maybe some day
in future times
and other crimes
that grab a kid
and give him pay
to beat on others
as the only way
to survive each day
on a gladiator's wage
entertaining the rich
on poverty's stage.

VACATION FOR WORKAHOLICS

The plan is to stop
planning and intending
and setting and seeking
goals because the goal is to rest
from goal seeking,
except *that* becomes a goal too.
So how do you reach a goal
without seeking it?
And how do you plan to stop
without stopping to plan
or intending to vacation
without vacating the intention,
or attain the rest
without arresting the attaining
or resettling new goals,
having gained the goal of not gaining?
Unless, of course, you just quit!

SLEEP

Blessed are you, Sleep.
You heal and rest
and provide excuses for everything:
laziness, forgetfulness, absent-mindedness,
mindlessness, no-mindedness,
stupors, stupefaction,
(but never matter-of-factions)
cupids, affairs, orgies, revenge
and just about anything
you can dream up not to do
when you are awake.
So why do they search
the world over and even beyond the stars
for your perfect escape
from this world,
from hard work,
from stressful goodness?
When there you are waiting
to start the late-night movies
with me in the leading role,
and even, come to think of it,
and best of all, waiting to run
that dreamy matinee... ZZZZ

WHEN THEY FINALLY LEAVE THE CHILDREN SO QUICKLY

When they finally leave,
the children so quickly,
a lonesome relief,
an endless, sudden, grinding, shattering,
joyous sadness,
so full of regrets and reprieves,
of might-have-beens and
from could-have-been worse-nesses
that we teeter between tears
of grace-faced remorse and
doom-shadowed ecstasy and
turn slowly to
the daring, delightful prospect that
we, for sake of earth's cycles and
a tinge of revenge,
might play again at our childhood
when they finally leave,
the children so quickly.

ZEALOT'S FAIR

I went to the zealot's fair.
It had a wild esprit.
The "truth" was told in every tent,
but none of them agreed.
Not only truth but right as well
was preached from every stall.
Each one sought a total faith,
blind soldiers dressed to fall.
Each denounced all evil ways.
They played upon my fears.
They appealed to goodness and fair play,
but hate leaked out their ears.
Perhaps it's better to choose one flag
and accept no substitute.
Confused by facts is worse than life,
a death of strong repute.
I walked on to the freak show.
It mocked our human flaws.
They held up creatures who worshipped God,
odd beings who chose no cause.
But these freaks of God did have a way
that pulls me by their care.
I'd sooner love than bash a foe
or stay at the zealot's fair.

FIRST GRANDSON, DYLAN

Spread-eagled in the bassinet
is where I first saw you,
sleeping off the cramped ordeal,
you kicked and slugged
the boundless, naked space.
In perfect powerlessness
you unite and reunite,
with your mighty innocent power,
the splits and tears
of family feelings.
And bind us by your weakness
to our soft side,
exposed,
by your every-sided
softness
that pulls out once hesitant
kindnesses and measured vulnerabilities,
wrecking our settled routines and
crashing through firm boundaries
with your teddy bear army,
your mountain of logistical support,
medical and press corps ready,
a revolution
overturning
the ancient regime.

BLOSSOMS

Apple petals lifted off
the tree by the May breeze
showering down to
the just-tilled garden,
catching in the rows
to make ragged lines
of white in the brown earth.
Like snow in the summer,
the beauty vanishes before I
can catch it.
I try to grasp the sweet grass
smoke spirit of native rites.
I cannot hold the spring,
I know,
but do not try to stop me.
Let me keep the
blossom storm in my heart
for the hard times of hot weeding
and anger I must take in now
as I leave the garden for
the more ragged brown and white world.

THE DREAMERS
(for Verna Rapp Uthman)

Your gaze is always far.
You hold onto the vision
and focus on a star.
Thank God for dreamers.
They don't see our faults,
at least they don't tell.
We need them to see the hope
when we struggle in our hell.
Without our lifted head
fixed on a juster way,
we'd focus on our weakness
and on our feet of clay.
Our dreams are not illusions.
They're clear and ripe for all.
We only have to see the way
and listen to the call.
Most don't see that star.
The sun has burned it out.
Busy with their daily deeds,
they forget what life's about.
God calls us dreamers
with gaze that's soft and fair.
To see that distant hope,
the star that's always there.

HURRICANE

A hurricane scatters homes
as if they were confetti,
and a storm of lies clutters
grim city streets
as politicians meet
to fog truth beyond bother.
We search out the roads
that define us.
Then we gather our tools
to build again
paper homes
that hope to shelter
brief moments of truth
and small spaces of trust.

WORK

When did fun become hard to have
or when was energy driven through
narrow channels
like a river dammed up
to force its flow
through turbines for purposes other
than simply going naturally down
from the mountains of high ecstasy
to the wild seas' deep, down darkness?
Well, work is the answer
to this and, sadly, most all questions.
Yes, work.
It gets you going
to power the wheels of industry,
to wheel the power of industry and
other important purposes

so darn well that you can't
remember the mountain thrills
or the ocean depths
except in dreams you must squelch
because
well, hell, you are lucky to
have work, right?
And further, because without it
how are you going to pay for
rides at the wet and wild
amusement park
if you ever have time off to go?

THE CHILD IN ME

There are the children, of course,
so evidently growing
far beyond my reach.
But there is also the child
in me who
is so close
I can't see him.
But he rages around
inside me at other's offenses,
purrs with satisfaction
at my indulgences
and turns cartwheels at rare enchantments
so that I, the cautious parent,
push so far away
that my orphan may,
with his silent outrages,
break me in
to let him out.

DEAD-BEATEN DAD

"Victim Dad Liable for Son's Defense in Kill Plot"

So the headlines read
and strange law decreed.
Dad, target of son's hate,
also trapped in legal fate.
Thus I feel with wayward son,
held in ransom for what he's done.
Popular view has dad so free
he can do all he would be.
But son holds tight
and drains his might.
Then law will secure
what he will endure.
Am I like him, a set up fool,
paying a fee to be a tool?
What's the way out of this trap?
Looking around, I find no map.
Advisors insist I lay him flat,
like telling the mouse to maul the cat.
Advice is cheap to dads who care,
but guides are few and wisdom is rare.
All I found is this way to frame.
What goes on can have a name.
Meaning is there though feelings are sad,
the other side of the dead-beaten dad.

THESE WOUNDED HEROES

Painful pride around the native circle
proclaims "21, 14, 8 years of sobriety",
followed by applause.
Raw wounds healing,
I listen and wonder but
can never know
what it means to be
bounty-hunted, removed, allotted,
reservationed, and so cheated, so broken
that my being in the bleeding circle
is a piece of the oppression.
Palefaced, I am yet included in the family wake
because the institution requires it,
and also because maybe this native people
always welcomed us,
having evolved 10,000 years of earthly love.
How strange such pain can
still care and even love.
They must have a medicine plant,
long extinct in Europe,
but still known
among these battered heroes
of the Mother we labeled
"America."

AT PONCA CREEK

At Ponca Creek
the Lakota still hold on,
among the Whites,
tightly webbed
in punctured communities,
connected to each other,
in the rolling hills,
the wooded valleys,
and the ceaseless wind.
The punctures of Wounded Knee
close to the West
and the thirty-eight hanged
all at once, close to the East,
the Natives still bleed for in their souls
ravaged by White conquest.
Yet there is joy in Ponca Creek
at kindnesses given,
at earth-born cycles of
prairie growth
and brown-eyed babies
less scared from these wounds
but too soon weary
of blue-eyed sportsmen at
Ft. Randall Dam
who may not think about
how much power they have
to crush the joy that
wants to seep out of this
land's renewing births.
How much of the desolation
will claim the bright child faces
singing Jesus Loves Me
in these junkyard places
we call "reservations"?

I watch elders hang onto dignity
in a silence so deep
it seems an eternity
before a smile
cracks a solemn mask
hardened by centuries of cold winds
and "treaties"
broken from the beginning,
even before the Hotchkiss guns
finished off the dancing ghosts
when that tattered band tried to run
at Wounded Knee, where the
Seventh Cavalry wounded us all.
Their silent rage fits the pain
though we hardly feel the shame
our dumb speech or sport
and mocking lore
cast over the dead buffalo plain
leaving our desolation at their door.

FORT BERTHOLD

There is no fort at Fort Berthold
Indian Reservation,
Nor any reserve
of outside intrusions.
The shattered road sign
at the entrance
endures bullet holes
as the three ancient tribes
(even the Arickara Scouts,
proud in their army uniforms,
returned from the Second War)
were moved from the flood waters
of the Garrison dam, that
would cut the heart out of them.
and out of the Mandan
and the Hidatsa farms and economy
now fifty feet deep down
under the lake of "progress"
and White recreation.
They stare down from the badlands buttes
in prefab houses barely surviving
along the offered road out:
assimilation.
There is no fort at Fort Berthold.
There is no need for it
below the water.

NOW

How could cabin fever
ever exist
when coming home
is so delicious?
Home jumps its welcome,
doors smile open
and the floor purrs
happiness on my feet.
Even the routine chores
shape my peaceful excitement,
for I am home now,
and the clanging alarm systems
are shut off with rich silence.
The radar alert warning
halts its dervish spin.
I am home now to the world
I have made to fit my mold.
Poured back now, I settle
in for healing and lazy days
of rest and the soul refueling
itch to escape
the fever-shrunk cabin.

ZERO TOLERANCE

When Americans
look back on
our time,
shame will grip
us for the many
cruelties we have wrought.
Highest among them
are the lowest attacks
on voiceless, innocent
children,
for they have no defense
when they are torn
from their parents.
That was our government's
policy to stop the
entry of more families
at our borders who are
"yearning to be free",
escaping the violence
of their homeland
only to find a heartless
family separation from this
"land of the brave and
home of the free."

FIREFLIES

The fireflies were our fireworks
again this Fourth.
A full moon added a light
to the field and trees
as we remembered
other Fourths so child-directed,
and expected.
Soon summers of our own
when the fireworks
inside us are plenty
to savor
and flavor life
better than a trip or show.
Having these enough,
I know
to look for the fire aglow
in your face,
for there I see
what is firefly to some
is fireworks to me.

GENE BY THE SEA
(for Gene Kuehl)

Your gifts to others
are rarely lavished on yourself,
except by the sea
where a gull's flight soars
out of your leather skin
lost for a time in eternity,
still like straight smoke,
so that cares, carried aloft,
can ascend a while
before
the wind and rush of duties
blow away your peace,
and your love of life
splashes you like a
cold wave, somewhat more
ready for love's burdens.

PRAYERS

ON TRYING TO PRAY

O Lord,

We are up against it when we try to pray.

Because in prayer we have to admit that we are not in power even though we may be praying for an immediate power play with ourselves on top.

When we pray to the gods, we at least confess that we need help from beyond ourselves, that we cannot do it alone.

But when we pray to You, our prayers for a raise, a new house, peace and quiet, kids that behave, for more appreciation, for damnation to our enemies, health and safe travel, it is hard to forget your saints who got no raises and were not known for their opulent wealth,

Thy apostles who had no place to lay their heads—no homes, children, peace or quiet, and Thy servant Paul who bore his infirmities and revolutionized the world.

And we find it particularly hard to avoid thinking of Jesus, who was not very safe and secure, who blessed his murderers, who was appreciated only when it was safe and the thing to do, and who, when he prayed, did not worry much about himself.

What can we pray for when we remember that You are the God of these people?

When we pray to You, how can we ask for more than Your saints had?

When we pray to You, we have already forsaken ourselves, said "yes" to

Your world, opened ourselves to the poor, the wretched, the sick, the destitute, the old, and the bereaved.

When we pray to You, we have declared that our lives are at the disposal of the future well-being of people, to the restless search for You and Your will for a dissatisfaction with anything that cheapens life, that degrades people, and that grants special privilege.

When we pray to You, we are never content when wars rage and bombs falls on villages in our name, when our nation polarizes itself between races, when people vegetate in front of a television tube— tired from inhuman competition for cheap successes.

When we pray to You, we are left with nothing but a gratitude for abundance, determination to change the world, courage to speak against injustice, and humility to control pretension.

When we pray to You, nothing is left for us but our souls and all is gained for You and Your kingdom.

When we pray to You, we are rid of all but what we need most—Thy will.

Thy will be done in the world as it is in heaven.

A PRAYER FOR AWE TOWARD THE AWESOME

Dear Lord,

We are fearfully grateful that our anxieties have not always been toward what was in our power to control:

For the secular courage to defy all superstitions, we are the benefactors,

For the holy mystique which drew scientists and scholars beyond the respectable, we are obligated,

For artists, playwrights, comedians and revolutionaries whose spirit drew them beyond the fringe, we are indebted,

For the small dreams and visions that thrill us uncelebrated people, we bow in gratitude.

For all those strengths that come despite our reason, regardless of facts and free of logic, the strength:

- to listen to one more learned than we are,
- to wait while time is precious,
- to fall into the night of sleep,
- to accept another problem,
- to receive again new mysteries in our associates,
- to be awed by the sea,
- to be consumed by passion,
- to be influenced by events,

Because of these we stand as rich people.

May we with our passive endowments remain actively free from all that would demean us.

May we stand free from all that is less than holy.

May daily problems not overwhelm us.

May we love our children but doubt their whims.

May we affirm our friends but question their faults.

May we find the sacred in the church and apart from it.

May we suspect, question, analyze, probe, scrutinize, investigate and bring before the light of day all that is not truly sacred, that we may serve only it and be free of all else.

For those who experience more closely the mystery of death, we share their bereavement.

For those whom the mysteries have overwhelmed and defeated, we pray for strength.

For those who have lost the spark to carry on, we beg its near advent.

For those for whom the holy is only superstition, we trust they might think the second mile.

For those bodies which are dying, return them to You, the ground of our confidence.

For those marriages that have rested on unholy grounds, revive them with sacred foundations.

And may nations and all the king's men some day learn that human power and machinery cannot put the mystery of life back together again.

Lord God, You have answered our question even in the asking.

For when we have forgotten You, You have remembered us.

For You fill the emptiness of our hearts, the missing part of our souls.

And though we are lifeless, having run out our willfulness, You are there pricking us alive and commuting our death wishes.

So revived and pardoned may we plead the case of others for whom we are now free to care.

Set Thy wonderment upon the despairing and Thy heavy hand upon the vain, that we may find a world at peace, that our nation may bear its power with compassion, that our community may wisely choose its course, that our educators may inform our youth of the many needs of the forsaken, that our church may show us what to do with our commitments, that the sick and mentally lame be made whole, and the bereaved know of our care in Your kingdom which we cannot fathom; but thanks be to You, we need not, for You have taught us that at least this one thing we need not understand.

These and many other things You made clear to us in the life, death, and prayers of Jesus, in whose image we pray.

PRAYER WHEN THINGS ARE FALLING APART

O Thou who hears our every groan and sigh of joy, we are in trouble, and we don't know how to get out of it.

We have taken charge of nature and we live in comfort but just staying comfortable takes all our time, so we seldom seem able to take charge of ourselves.

We have a goal of the best of all political processes—granting, we thought, equality and opportunity to all, but something went wrong.

And we are faced with burning cities and warfare in our streets.

We intend only to live in peace with other nations and are even vigorous in its pursuit by protecting small countries who are pushed around. But we found war not so simple, our protection not always wanted; and we are severely tempted to destroy every bit of humanity in those we want to protect and in ourselves.

Even as pressing perhaps is our inability to ask for help. To come right to the tragic point, God, we cried "Lord, Lord" but went right on assuming that technology, our economic system, and the sword were really all that finally counted.

We have sought to better the world with our great discoveries, but have forgotten that one thing that was needful: humility toward what we are really up against. We even forgot the language of prayer -- we do not really pray much.

Yet we have not lost everything. We still cry out for justice. We can yet sigh for joy. We groan when sorrowful. We can laugh at a good joke that catches us off guard. Our tongues even slip into a word of praise or damnation. We still gasp at sublime beauty. We even sometimes bow our heads at wondrous skills displayed and occasionally in a rare moment crawl down on our cracking knees to say with our bodies what will not come in our words.

Thank God we have not lost everything. Struggling, agonizing to some honesty, we work our way to the beginning of our lost language of prayer because the prayerful awareness of our limits still remains for God's sake.

Our words will be slow to come, Lord; for if we are honest and babble prayers like some recipes and magical mumbo jumbo, we surely have lost even that last thread of hope.

Meanwhile we sigh and groan because we truly need help. The pretty worlds we built needlessly are falling to pieces.

Knowing our limits, we groan, we sigh, and we smile at a yet remaining mystery which we do not control.

DIFFICULTY OF PRAYER

Lord God, toward whom we have come to feel as strangers, we find it very hard to pray because whether we do or not life seems to go on:

Wars are fought.

The laundry gets done.

Loans are taken out.

Children cry and sleep.

Some of us wonder if anyone is listening when we pray.

We are not sure whether You have left us alone or if that we are dead to Your nearness.

The more we learn about the world, the less we seem to know about what can pull us out of our destitution.

Deep in our souls we are aware that something is missing.

We don 't know what it is but we seem to have lost it somewhere between puberty and old age, between new science and Robert Oppenheimer, between the priesthood of all believers and anarchy of most spectators, between Appomattox Courthouse and the Bay of Aqaba, between "Now I lay me down" and "this god-awful traffic".

Yet we are at ease calling thy curses upon our enemies.

Why can we not seek Thy blessing even for our friends?

Why can we not say "Thy will be done?" Is it because we must forsake our own?

Why can we not say with our hearts what we mumble with our lips: "Give us this day our daily bread"? Is it because we have too much bread, too easily gotten?

Why can we not pray "make us to forgive our debtors" as well as we sentence misfortune by saying "He had It coming"?

Why can we not center down on the core of our lives which we may not control rather than scattering ourselves to the peripheries of our self-projections?

Lord God, you have answered our questions even in the asking.

For when we have forgotten You, You have remembered us.

For you fill the emptiness of our hearts, the missing part of our souls.

And though we are lifeless, having run out our willfulness, You are there pricking us alive with our discomfort.

And though we fall weary of too much discomfort, You are there comforting us commuting our death wishes.

So, revived and pardoned may we plead the case of others for whom we are now free to care.

Set Thy wonderment upon the despairing and compassion for the weak.

In Jesus' name, amen.

LORD, WE WOULD BE GOOD IF IT WERE EASY

O Thou who makes fools of our heroes and saints of our fools,
We would be good if it were easy.
We would be humble if it were more glamorous.
We would be sacrificial if it paid off.
We would be kind if it were reciprocated.
We would be zealous if it gave prestige.
We would forsake our privileges if we got credit.
We would stand up for the poor if they would appreciate it.
We would speak out against wrong if it were in good taste.
We would fight for justice if we could keep our jobs.
We are ready to give our all, Lord, if You will give it back at 4½%.
I think You understand our problem, Lord.

- It's just that, well, we do have to eat.
- Well, no, not steak every night but we can't risk our children's future.
- Yes, I know Jesus said that one "who loves son or daughter more than me is not worthy of me."
- Ha, ha! of course He did not really mean that literally.
- He did?
- Yes, but Jesus had all that fame and honor and glory.
- Of course, there was that part about the crucifixion.
- What do You want us to be anyway, do-gooders or something?
- You do?
- Well, what if we just give up our lives for great causes and no one knows about it?
- You will?
- I suppose that's enough, Lord.

DRAWING THE LINE

Lord,
Thank You for oiling our souls and cooling our heels.
Thank You for biting our tongues and trying to listen.
Thank You for second winds and extra miles.
Thank You for forgetting our indignations and ending our grudges.

Lord,
Sometimes our resentments choke us down and it gets so stuffy in
our souls that we are ready to clobber the first person who we know
can't hit us back.
Turn us on to Thy graces and help us to react to the right people
and causes.
Help us to say what later we think we should have said.
Help us to fear nothing, to draw the line where it can
preserve the soul.
Help us to not endure what we cannot laugh at and help us to laugh
at what would intimidate us if we did not trust You.
Trusting in You, we can come through because no one can threaten
us with losing our jobs, we are not afraid of what people think, and
we cannot be bought or sold since we are indebted only to You.

Lord,
We will meet a thousand offers to sell out this week:
    to hatred
    to violence
    to gossip
    to aggressive friends
    to goofy ads, cheap gimmicks, and political propaganda
    to "secure" futures "safe" residences
    to expedient compromises and prudent standards.
Clean our souls, Lord, so we can dirty our hands to risk just actions,
    and save us from the graceless one who would gain us the world
    but lose us our souls

SAVE US FROM PERFECTION

Lord, save us from utopias.

The rulers make gods of what is and the rebels make idols of what will be.

Lord, take away our false gods.

We want maximum choice and minimum accountability.

Lord, give us only the responsibility we can handle.

Lord, we are inundated by media which simplify everything.

But most of our kids are simply kids, which means they are not simple.

And some of us do not fall for all that cheap fun, and we do have causes that are not always for ourselves.

Lord, save us from simplicity and neutrality.

Make our souls rest so much in You that we are forced to cut loose from our riches.

Make us give total commitment only to Thee so that we will not take ourselves so seriously or our enemies so fearfully.

And make us fall for You, so we won't sell out to anything and make us love the world as it is so we can make it become what it can be.

ON DEATH

Oh God,
Death stalks us every day in our wars.

It kills our expectations and attacks our curiosity, but most painful
is death's claim on our leaders whom we come to love too late and
too casually.

Lift us, O God, beyond the morbid pity of death's fascination to the
life of Thy self-emptied servants.

Lift us beyond the end that death brings us to the possibility that
life gives us.

May we transcend our times and needs and focus on the eternal cries
of the needy.

Let us listen to our poor so that we act in defense of more than
ourselves.

Inspire our leaders to see beyond election day and incite us who
follow to see before election day that our timid leaders lean so much
on our worst desires.

Finally, when our own death comes, let it be that some good will
live after us, that some people are better off because of us, that some
useful structure endured in spite of us, that some peace was won
because some wars were stopped, that some lives were saved through
us because death's claim on us had lost its frightfulness.

So that when we die, we will not die alone for we will rest then with
those who emptied themselves of private needs and filled others with
public good.

TO THE SPIRITS

O spirit of goodness, hope and love, we are grateful that You are present to us on occasion. Of course, we like to take all the credit for it, saying that "We are good, we are hopeful, we are loving." One reason for doing such a boorish thing is that we seem to think that we need all the credit we can get in order to please You. So, we sit around half of our lives counting up all of our good points like puppy lovers in love with ourselves never realizing that goodness, hope, and love are free gifts, never resting on the desperate hope of pulling ourselves into goodness by our own bootstraps.

O spirit of faith, courage and compassion, we are grateful for Your presence to us on occasion because we are so often possessed by unfaith, cowardice, and indifference. Such demons make us act like savages, and we wonder whether or not we have come very far from the apes. All we are sure of is that we are sometimes neater in killing our brother than Cain. He had to look Abel in the eye. We simply pay taxes.

O spirit of achievement, protect us from success and rationalization and attempted self-justification of our accomplishments which become the ends of our toil while the means, being ruthless, leave no room for humility.

O spirit of self-sacrifice and nobility, protect us from self-righteous crusades and self-certain causes. We have been wrong so many times that our self-esteem seems to be preserved only by the demon of pride. Relieve us of the need for self-indulgence and make us proud of thee.

O spirit of joy, preserve us from base flights from the needs of others. Bored with a million crying souls, we seek thrills on a mountain slope, in new gadgets, tempting inebriation, and dreaming our lives away. Make our joy be in the hungry fed, the naked clothed, the sick healed, and the insane inspired with the spirit of all our joy--that of Jesus Christ.

A GRACE

O Thou but for whose grace we would be famished each day of our
lives as so many are in our world,
Many are confronted by hunger, sickness, and poverty at all times,
but especially in war.
And when there is some taste of that hunger and war near at home,
it becomes a heavy burden for all sensitive people.
Our joy is tempered by others' suffering.
Our health is measured against their disease.
Our comfortable homes are made uncomfortable,
Our food, tasteless.
Our money, ill-gotten.
Our children, spoiled.
Our learning, arrogance.
Our security, stifling.
Our imaginations, dulled.
Our feelings, numbed.
With the same undeserving grace which rewards us rather than
others with all material abundance, bless us with the ever-greater
abundance of joy at others' good fortune:
healthy souls and pure consciences,
comfort in another's well-being,
food for our sick spirits,
money to give to the poor,
children to become servants of humankind,
learning and thought to untangle our self-deceptions.
security when all are at peace.
And if our feeling becomes so dead that we expect or demand our
next meal because we deserve it more than a needy child who does
not seem to worry about our American honor, then chasten us and
deny us and prick us to be alive to hungry stomachs and filled souls.
We have done nothing to earn this feast before us. May we do much
because it has been given to us.

A CHRISTMAS PRAYER

O Lord,

We want to say that despite what we have been, we desire to be different.

Despite our eagerness to receive presents, we wish also to give gifts.

Despite our inability to be truly grateful, we want to give thanks.

Despite our greedy expectations, we would like to rejoice even at the most inappropriate gift.

Despite our unhappily scrambling to match gifts received, we would like to make another happy also.

Despite our efforts to capture the Christmas spirit with tinseled trees and toy guns, we try to surrender to the Christian spirit, perhaps only in the melancholy feelings after the last gift is opened.

Despite our great abundance and unnecessary spending, we occasionally remember some people actually starve for lack of care.

We know all of this. That is more or less why we are here, and we remember that Old St. Nicholas never writes us letters about what he wants, but he seems much happier than we are when his bag is empty.

We pray now that You make us able
- to give more than we receive and to receive whatever we are given,
- to be grateful at merely having what we have and full of joy at receiving more,
- to love our parents and not feel sorry for their too useful gifts,

- to love our children and not feel hurt by their honesty.

For despite what might appear to be our desires, oh Lord, we do want to look beyond the Christmas tree lights to the star that shines over One who had very little to be thankful for, but gave His life in gratitude, who had few toys, but had a more joyous life, who later had not even a place to sleep, but rejoiced at the sight of birds in the air and lilies in the field, who had all the problems we have and more because He seemed to suffer at other's pain, but whose heartache was not self-pity, and died even for those who could only pity themselves.

And if our feeling becomes so dead that we expect or demand our next meal because we deserve it more than a needy child who does not seem to worry about our American honor, then chasten us and deny us and prick us to be alive to hungry stomachs and filled souls.

We have done nothing to earn this feast before us. May we do much because it has been given to us.

A PRAYER FOR RECOGNITION OF A MINISTER TO A CHURCH

O Thou who looked upon the way things are and said: "It is good", separate us from our illusions that we might be true and real to ourselves and to You and so receive Your good blessing.

For we are those who make of these good things, tools of our needs and false hopes out of our despair. We, therefore, need Your sight which can carry us beyond our shortsightedness to see the truth of the way things are.

Especially we dare to hope that You will be present to our new pastor so she will more often have Your sight and therefore see it like it is and see us as we are.

Help her to see the false struggle for our sacred cows and declare only our struggle for the sacred to be good.

Help her to see in our almost endless committee meetings the yearning for true representation and organization and declare that yearning to be good.

Help her to see the cries for more simplicity, less simplicity, more relevance, less relevance, more soothing comfort, and less self-righteous dissent to be cries for communication, communion, and even love and to declare these to be good.

Help her to see in the constant pressure to do almost everything and do it yesterday or else, an appeal to her usefulness and declare it good.

Help her to see in our need to make her a "good" woman, a more "religious" woman, our appeal for help to be maturely human ourselves. And may she declare that appeal to be good, setting her free from us and open to You, that she may not depend upon us to tell her to work or to rest that she may not depend upon us to tell her she is loved, that she may not depend upon us to study, that she may not depend upon us to be too weak or too strong.

May her eyes see and in seeing, sparkle with affection for our true selfhood and may her frown pain our false pretensions.

May her prayers be poetry.

May her sermons be psalms to the people.

May her presence be a merciful dance of critical love.

Finally, we dare to ask what we have wanted for all along and know in our strong moments to be enough: that you be with her to lift her beyond her weakness and to humble us to see You in her and be able to declare that your presence is what we need.

AN EASTER PRAYER

Christ, You made it. We thought You were dead. We kill Your body with religious rules and Roman swords, but You rise up in a law of love and weapons of mercy, for we see You in the apostles who change the world because You did not die.

Christ, You made it. We thought You were dead. We kill Your body with inquisitions and crusades, but You rise up in peaceful monks and vagabond preachers. For we see You in Francis, Thomas, and Luther who change the world because You did not die.

Christ, You made it. We thought You were dead. We kill Your body with scientism and dogmatic reaction, but You rise up in relativity and a self-critical church. For we see You in a humbled science and a missionary church which change the world because You did not die.

Christ, You can make it. We keep thinking You are dead. We are killing Your body with technological warfare, but You are rising up in world of law and a community of nations. For we are seeing it in treaties and peace-makers who are changing the world because You did not die.

Christ, You can make it. We keep thinking You are dead. We are killing Your body with slavery, segregation, and the ghetto, but You are rising up in non-violence, for we have seen You in 3,000 lynchings: Medger Evers, and Martin Luther King, Jr., the Kennedys, and George Floyd, who are changing our nation because You will not die.

Christ, You can make it. We keep thinking You are dead. We grieve over our loved ones who are torn from us taking much of us with them. We see our children in cages. We are told that most of the world is hungry. We know of lonely strangers, prisoners, and sick friends. We play with Your church as if it were a penny arcade of cheap religious thrills needing only our holiday tips.

Will You rise now, Christ?

He seems to be saying He will rise if we raise up the love for others that our loved ones had for us.

He will rise if we raise up the undeserved love we miss so much and give it to the undesirable ones who need it so much.

He will rise if our paternal charity will become fraternal love.

He will rise if our property rights will wait for human rights.

He will rise if our human conventions will step aside for human dignity.

He will rise if our business as usual will become mutual concern.

He will rise if our eyes will open to see Him in the hungry, oppressed, and the lonely; and our energies will burst forth in new resurrections that change the world now, because He will not die.

Christ, you <u>will</u> make it again if You will help us.

I think he is saying He will!

A PRAYER FOR A GOOD DAY

Lord, it is a good day, isn't it?

It is so good that we want to say so.

It is good because we really can appreciate our own worth and since bold acts of courage are now possible for us.

It is good because each of us is simply a wonderful person due to the fact that, well, due to the fact that, I started to say, "We had it coming", but I am glad I didn't say that. It would not be very humble, but most of all, it would not be true.

To tell the truth, we don 't know why we have the courage to affirm ourselves, and that ignorance is very humbling.

So, it also is a very fine day, isn't it, Lord, because we can be humble too and since compassionate acts of sacrifice are now possible for us.

It is good because each of us is simply a humble, self-sacrificing person due to the fact that, well, due to the fact that, I started to say, we are "swell people", but I am glad I didn't say that either. It would not be very courageous, but most of all it would not be true.

Yet it's a good day anyway, isn't it, Lord?

It may sound like we're hedging now, Lord, but not every day seems all that good to us. Just every once in a while, well quite often, we get to be cowards thinking that we are humble and then we hate ourselves for getting pushed around and we spend a lot of time making speeches about what we should have said to some wise guy. That's what I call a bad day. It's rather hard to ask for courage; it seems so humiliating. But, just in case, we sure do need more backbone, Lord.

And then there are the days when we mistake bold, inconsiderate blunders for courage. "I am tired of being at the tail end," we say. But then we spend the rest of the day feeling guilty for hurting some poor person who was only trying to help, and we cover our guilt by saying he had it coming. That is also what I call a bad day. It's rather hard to ask to be more humble; it's bold to ask that, but we do need some humility rather badly, Lord.

We need these things because all kinds of people are crying all over themselves, whining and complaining, nagging and pitying themselves so much that it must sound like a world full of cats to you, Lord. Well, they do not need us to add to their complaints, Lord. They could use some of our courage--I mean they could use courage wherever it comes from. Maybe we would make a very strong effort to get out of the way so that these folks might get a lift.

We often think that some people have a right to pity themselves because there seems to be no lack of other people that specialize in meanness and fights, but we can try to keep brutality from winning the day. These mean ones could use some of our humility. No, that's not right. I mean meanness should be humbled wherever it comes from. Maybe we could make a very bold attempt to get out of the way so that the proud may fall without a bounce.

Anyway, we know of One who did these things one very good day.

ON USING THE TIME WE ARE GIVEN

O You who brings wisdom to our knowing and destruction to our pretended knowledge,

You have given each of us three score and ten or twenty years. What will we do with it, Lord?

In that time which we did not earn, we are freely granted all we need for life. What will we do with it, Lord?

We are given parents. Will they become our excuse for failure, or will we approve them in spite of their deeds, freeing us to deeds unneedful of approval?

We are given friends. Will we use them to flatter and agree with us, or will we be used by them to do the needful thing?

We are given education. Will we employ it for more and greater privileges or will we consider it to be a tool for seeking justice and mercy?

Some of us are given white skin. Will we pretend that it is superior and suppose we deserve the privileges we inherited, or will we be strong enough to declare that all races are superior and that we need not meekly depend upon our whiteness to afford us advantages?

We are given a church. Will we fortify its walls with self-protection, or will we open its doors and commission its people to protect others: the poor, the hungry, sick, and those in prison?

Get us out of ourselves, Lord, out of thinking that our gifts are earned and disposable like some empty bottles of soda.

Let us not abuse our gifts or ourselves but use them for others; and when church, skin pigment, education, friends, and all the other abundance we have is emptied on others may we rest from our efforts aware that our time also was a gift about whose conclusion we will have no regrets.

ON BEING A FOOL

O You who are unknown by us but ever present to us, we are so often fools for the devil.

Foolishly we depend upon the deeds of hucksters to be trustworthy.

We are grateful that we need only find trust in you to put meaning into our commerce.

Foolishly we count upon mass communication to be objective. We are grateful that we need only find faith in Thee who draws us on to communicate the truth.

Foolishly we are impressed by technology and production to make us even more comfortable. We are thankful that we need only be impressed by what stimulates us to craft and creation.

Foolishly we are awed by people of prestige. We are thankful that we need only be awed by You to whom all of us are prestigious.

Foolishly we trust in the wisdom of politicians and expect their righteousness. Thank goodness our final trust need only be in Thee whose rule frees us to political maturity and action.

Foolishly we depend upon ourselves to be in charge on every occasion.

Thanks to Thee, we need only depend on You to take charge of us.

Foolishly we place our faith in all the humanly manufactured institutions, personalities and contraptions when we trust so little to Your unknown power.

Strengthen us to be foolish only toward You, but to be critically suspect of everything else, and give us the grace to know the difference.

PRAYER FOR VISIONS

O You who teaches us through visions which make our spirits soar and who teaches us through reality that dashes our pretensions, we seek the vision and the courage to face the real so that we may be grateful for our lives.

In hope of such gifts we try to express our thanks for what is and for vision to see what might be.

We have been blessed with abundance, but with vision we will seek ultimate solace in You.

We have been blessed with parents, but with vision seek our parenthood from You.

We have been blessed with brothers and sisters, but with vision we know that all persons are our brothers and sisters.

We have been blessed with children, but with vision we know that they are not our possessions.

We have been blessed with a stable government, but with vision we see its potential instability.

We measure our attitudes against those of faith who express thy will, and we find our faith is weak and our efforts self-seeking.

We pray for eyes to see reality in pained faces in the teeming cities with thwarted minorities, in the lonely, hollow bodies of the forgotten elderly, in the frightened stares of the insane, in the sightless stare of the dead, in the fragile glances of the developing young, and in the pathetic sight of the mean and cruel.

And we pray for courageous vision always to see beyond our doubts to the possibility of strong faith and selfless giving.

Now we pray Thy intercession of grace upon our souls yearning for peace but barricaded with defenses, upon our tasks which seek to contribute but are too eager to compete, upon our families which seek to grow together but too often fall apart, upon our church which seeks to inspire but too often is served only by duty, upon our schools which seek to inform but too often only make us conform, upon our newspapers and publishers who would enlighten but are too often too eager to sell, upon our adult students who would continue to grow but are tempted with stale thoughts and sluggish sayings, upon our civic leaders who would serve the public good but are attracted to private greed, upon our national leaders who would bring peace, but are blinded by national pride.

Especially we pray for guidance in our wars-- may our policies be strategies for peace.

Take away our idolatry of nationalism that we may learn to cooperate with international laws.

Restore our world to peace and remind us that if we live by the sword we shall surely die by it.

Fill the nations of the world with justice and freedom from want and let us war no more.

These petitions and intercessions we ask and measure against the truly selfless life of Jesus the Christ.

ON ILLEGAL LAWS AND LEGAL FREEDOM

Lord,

Thank you for laws, for fences, for order, for structure, for boundaries when we assume that life is our private merry-go-round and we are drunk with free rides.

Thank you for freedom, boundlessness, chaos, and disorder when we assume that life is a maze of rules and earnable merit badges, and we are fatigued with its regimented paces.

Thank you for children who laugh at our laws and make us feel like policemen and executioners, for animals who jump fences, for the wind that changes its mind, for all the unpredictable confusions that free us to confession of our confused predictions.

Thank you for rules, regulations, cops and patterns and models and plans and streets and hedges, gates and table manners and straight-laced grandmothers who make us feel like libertines and pigs; for clocks, time schedules and for all the people who come on time and all the time that comes to assure us that people will have order.

Free us from absolute laws imposed on our guilt alone and from relative laws obeyed if we feel like it. Bind us to feeling and willing to choose our own orders so we may so rule ourselves.

May we be on time, Lord.

May we be ready and may we do our homework.

May we discipline ourselves so that others will not have to make special provision in case we sleep late.

Let us choose the patterns and institutions and laws we enjoy instead of complaining about their restrictions, or if we must complain, give us the grace to let it go.

Lord, rule again our churches so that we may be free to fail and bound to succeed in speaking and acting the great news of legal freedom. End our conspiracy of mutual sloth.

Forgive our missed appointments so that we may admonish and forgive our brothers and sisters who do not carry their weight.

May our towns and state be ruled by timely laws, fair judges, and alert legislation. Unburden them from structures that serve only a few people so that they may order public affairs to suit the governed.

May our nation find orderly change in our changing order and be free to serve those whose justice is overdue. Free our nation and others from the pretension that rules need not prevail among countries and that ideologies are above law.

Free our people and all people to forsake competitive pride and bring us to a world free to live with of law and order.

ON THE GENERATION GAP

Lord, thank You for youthful irreverence that frees us from the mistakes of our elders, letting us make our own errors.

Thank you for mature humility formed by mistakes that help us endure the blunders of youth.

Give us all a true awareness of other's pain for which we are accountable so that we will have compassion for them.

And grant us all a dissatisfaction with injustice so that we will have courage to change.

Amen

A PRAYER FOLLOWING ANOTHER POLITICAL ASSASINATION

Lord, we need You, for while we were busy with other things, we awoke again to the racking news that our destinies are not in our hands, that our leaders walk precarious paths, that our political system is vulnerable, that our routines are always subject to your judging power.

Lord, we need You, for while we were busy with other things, we immediately sought—after solutions to our violence—gun control and crime prevention, and some perhaps with an appeal to a non-existent, peaceful past.

We reached for explanations from reporters whom we expect to be philosophers and theologians, and they answered.

We grasped at quick, medical reports from physicians with crucial but sterile anatomy lessons and they replied.

Lord, we need you, for while we were busy with other things, we were back to our routines, before noon.

The media had resumed its quiz shows, violent westerns and doctor dramas.

Not because we were insensitive but because our habits and lives have long pretended that we were in charge of all things, the new world and its changes caught us off guard. We were not ready.

So, Lord, we need You who make us ready, for we were busy with other things.

We are grateful for the limits You put upon us which empower us mightily to limit that pretension and renew our intention to make a safer world.

It is in You where our destinies rest.

It is by You that a leader holds power.

It is from You that our nation gains riches and thus its obligations, and it is to You that we return in our liveliness and in our death.

Aware of this and thy life-giving power, we fervently pray for the souls of our martyrs and re-dedicate our lives, energies, thoughts and feelings to a humble respect for the delicacy of life and a determination to discipline our lives for the protection, nourishment, and fulfillment of this frail thread of life in all people that You have given to us.

Only our wonder at Your gift of life gives us the energy to do what is necessary to end violence and madness of war.

Only when we see Your abiding grace can we have the courage to remain sensitive to the daily horror that is now televised for us.

Only when we place our destiny in Your care can we place our desire for good in others besides ourselves.

Only when we find our national blessing to be a precarious obligation can we fruitfully share our abundance.

And only when we discover our lives to be an undeserved gift, can we give them selflessly to humankind.

For while we were busy with other things, we find that after all You are still busy with us.

ON DEATH

O Thou who has dominion over death and who calls us to live free of death's strong grasp, we who do not always hear this call and who die long before we expire or suffer over much for loved ones long since protected in Your care, we need Your help again.

Loosen the knots in our throats, the lonely aches in our hearts, the fearful silence of an absent one and the constricting torment when our bodies seem not ready to carry on.

And permit us a beginning gratitude for a pain soon ending. Permit us gratefulness for a life far better lived when we have faced what is far worse than death -- that is, the dread of death which makes a dark night of all our days

Permit us to be thankful for the healing by those things that make death bearable and life a joy: for time whose passage bears our griefs away, for friends who help carry our load, for courageous saints and martyrs and soldiers whose defiance of the dark one encourages our love of the daylight to be more carefree.

And most of all, for the words, life, and courageous death of Jesus, who makes our problems and sorrows pale and small because of the large strength with which He bore His cross.

We know He is not dead when we see His spirit resurrected in our restored lives, when we see another's unrewarded sacrifice, or simply when life comes to us as good.

Join our aims, desires, and purposes to this One who gave us life by losing it, that we may be resurrected to full consciousness of life as it is.

Revive us to a vital lust for life that we may so love each moment that its passing is unnoticed in our next commitment.

Refresh our courage to dream the impossible and to try the ideal.

Release us from the graves of suspicion and anxiety to a place of wise trust and open care.

Unleash our world from the demonic madness of war to the holy madness of peace for which we will sacrifice much.

Teach us the harder virtues of compassion that does not strike back, of justice that plays no favorites, of patience which disciplines our outbursts that feel so good but accomplish so little, of peace making which needs no justification, of a willingness to forgive another when our grudges and self-pity are so comfortable, of defenselessness which is already fortified with the freedom to die for the sake of another.

For so we see the One who sought no protection for Himself. His only defense was His humble courage. But this is all He needed for He lives. He lives in our hearts!

A GRACE

Prepare us to receive Thy blessings, O Lord
obvious to us in food and friends,
Hidden from us in failure and burdens.
Give us graciousness toward the obvious gifts
and courage to receive Your hidden benefits.

YOUNG PEOPLE'S PRAYER

Lord, we offer thanks to You that we have the energies to do the many exciting tasks of each day, but please give us patience to wait for the older ones who take a little longer.

We are grateful for the quickness of perception that is our gift, but help us not to be upset at our parents who cannot read our minds.

We have many joys with people our own age, but save us from the tyranny of always doing what is fashionable.

Help us to do something because it is simply needed even though we do not get any credit for it.

Lord, we are thankful for all the conveniences of our lives even though we seem to our elders always to take them for granted.

Help us to be willing to be uncomfortable when something more important than a new car is at stake, like justice and peace.

And with all this knowledge we are attaining, let us learn something about life in the process.

We are grateful for all the discoveries and the educational opportunities we have, help us just once in a while to ask why.

Please keep these gifts in their proper perspective for us--may they be to us only tools to help relieve the agony of others, rather than little rewards that make us better than them.

And, Lord, we dare now ask that we slow down in our mad scramble to get somewhere, but help us occasionally to realize that life is for living and that everything is not going to be solved when we get out of school, or get to the top of our department, or become manager, or read one more book.

Give us the graciousness to accept what comes each day and the courage to fight very hard for what seems, after serious consideration, to be the right. But please never let us forget that the foolish person also thinks he or she is right.

So, when our great love for humanity leads us to start hating people, give us the good sense to leave them alone.

THANK YOU FOR CHILDREN

Lord,

Thank you for children.

When we are about to freeze all chances of breaking old habits, You send us children.

They give us another chance to face our limits because they are so honest, and they give us another chance to mobilize our possibilities because they need us.

Children are our second chance to be alive because they make us so uncomfortable with being dead.

Lord, we are afraid of the young because they know us too much and we control them too little.

Make us fearless of their knowledge and therefore free to correct their errors.

We avoid the young because they mirror back to us painful reflections of ourselves.

Make us to be what we demand of them, instead of saying it so much.

Help us to teach them to accept themselves by our love for them.

Help us to teach them to affirm life by our openness to it.

Help us to teach them to serve others by being servants ourselves.

Help us to teach them to find wholeness by our being whole.

Help us to teach them to find fulfillment through our contentment.

Help us to teach them to honor the weak and innocent by our respect for them.

O Lord, help our young to value only what is important, and strengthen us to be models for their teaching.

Save the young from our attempts to live through them.

Save them from our efforts to make them correct our mistakes, so that when they in turn come to the limits of their own lives and have to face their young and their own deaths, may we have shown to them an adequate model of courage that they may be up to these severe demands.

ON FACING UNPLEASANT FUTURES

Lord,

We accept your world with lumps in our throats, empty feelings in our stomach, and tears in our eyes because we partly know that accepting your world means that we do not even want comfort anymore. We are like a raw wound sensitive not to ourselves but for others. It means death to all our security and whatever the future brings.

The other part is worse (or best) when we accept Your world. We don't even know what is up next. That is what is so frightening; we are not in charge of tomorrow. So, it is very hard to accept what we cannot control. In fact, we are not so sure we want all that indefiniteness and insecurity, much less all that suffering and ugliness, all that hard work and discipline, all that embarrassing involvement that is required.

To be very frank, Lord, you really put it to us. Can't we be just simple, happy people with families and friendly neighbors that are our kind of folks?

All right, all right we know that stuff about neighbors, Samaritans and all, but we are not very important people. Even if we had the courage, you know, you can 't fight city hall.

Oh, I'm sorry. I did not mean that, but You have to admit it is hard.

You don't?

Well, we do have to feed our kids and see that they are educated.

Other kids?

Well, let their parents take care of them.

They don't?

Well, if they did not live like pigs, they could make something of themselves and their children's lives.

I am sorry I raised my voice. But we are having a hard time as it is. We can't worry about everybody in the world. Enough is enough.

It isn't?

Well, how much is enough? You want everything, don't You? Our hearts, minds, souls, and strength? Yes, we know we were warned but we didn't read the small print.

That why we are not so sure about how much good we can do.

We don't have to be sure? You mean we just try?

Try to open up to your world? Your dead, dying, sick, arrogant, bereaved, poor, hurt, belligerent, naive, naked, in prison, hungry, and thirsty?

Well, we do need help.

You will?

I guess then we're ready, Lord.

THE MASTER OF THE DANCE

Christ, You have asked us to sing:

To sing the gladness of your goodness,

To sing of the weakness of death,

To sing of the defeat of hate,

To sing of the success of weakness,

To sing of the power of a smile,

To sing of the glamour of just fooling around and being freely ourselves.

May our lives sing (like Yours) love songs to our enemies.

Christ, You have invited us to dance.

You danced into the lives of some nobodies and made them rich with your music.

You danced before all the lawyers with words of lawless love.

You danced to the sacred tunes of another world we could barely hear through the noise of our compromises with this world.

You danced to silent sounds before the state, refusing to march with its armies.

May we begin to hear that music and turn ourselves loose to reveling in your grace.

Christ, You are encouraging us to walk:

To walk into the hells you endure to heal tormented minds,

To walk out of our paralyzing fear that keeps us crippled
and ashamed,

To walk where other people avoid, trying not to be different,

To walk without our religious crutches, our superstitious limps,
our humiliated shuffles.

You have asked us to walk with you to the cross and to die for
God by serving our brothers and sisters.

By singing and dancing and walking and dying for us,
You have set the pace for us to die for You.

Help us to see that we never live or die for nothing.

May our something be no less than You.

COME ON LORD, SLOWLY

Jesus,
You came once with love instead of hate, peace in spite of the sword,
justice before order.
Are You going to come again?
Are we better prepared this time for Your visitation?
Will You weep over our cities now?
Will You find Your churches a den of robbers or a house of prayer?
Will we hang on Your every word or will we hang You on the
nearest tree?
Will You come to us in disguise not telling us of Your authority?

Lord,
We could use a little more time to get ready.
We have only had two thousand years, but I guess we are as ready as
we will ever be.
In fact, we could use Your help for we can never be ready without
love, hope, peace and justice.
Help us to make our cities livable.
Help us to worry more often about eternal things.
Help us to attend to Your words and to look for You in
every disguise.

LORD, YOU KNOW WE LOVE YOU

Lord, you know we love You.

You have given us beautiful children and eyes to insist upon
that beauty.

Give us also the gift to be their parents.

Lord, you know we love You.

You have given us a church community in which they can learn about
You. Now help us also to learn.

Lord, You know we love You.

You have given us Bibles that we give to our children in Your name.
Now help us to become familiar with Your Word.

Lord, You know we love You.

You gave us the law that we teach our children.

Help us to learn it too.

Lord, You know we love You.

You gave us prophets whose names our children learn.

Make us also hear their judgments.

Lord, You know we love You.

You gave us Jesus, whom our children sing about, to follow.

Help us give them not only songs, but lives to follow.

Lord, You know we love You.

You gave us the disciples whose sacrifices we tell to our children.

Make us now Your disciples who are ready to follow.

Lord, You know we love You.

NOW, LORD

O Thou who was willing to die for others and who therefore lives eternally, grant us that willingness thus to forsake ourselves.

Help us to give up grasping after our immortal futures so that we may more gracefully live in the mortal present.

Keep before us the limit of our time on earth so that we may drink in the wonders of each day.

Keep before us the limit of our powers so that what we <u>can</u> do 'Thy will be done'.

Keep before us the limit of our importance so that we will find more value in others.

Keep before us the limit of our loved ones' time on earth so that we will affirm them more while they are with us.

Keep before us the limit of our knowledge so that we will assert ourselves more humbly.

Keep before us the limits of our leaders so that we will speak to them more courageously.

And, Lord, remind us of our unlimited hopes.

Remind us that only what counts will live.

Only love will persist.

Only justice will continue.

Only mercy will transcend life.

Only peace will finally endure.

Lord, refresh these qualities in our loved ones who have died, so that we will let them safely rest with You. And renew these eternal values in us so that we may be willing, like You, to forsake our own lives and thereby live eternally with You.

WE ARE TIRED, LORD

Lord,

It may seem strange, because we have comfortable lives, but we too labor and are heavy laden and need rest.

Give us rest.

Give us the yoke of Christ which is light.

We carry the burdens of wanting to save the world, but we have not yet succeeded. Give us rest.

We carry the guilt of past mistakes but our habits are strong and we are afraid. Give us rest.

We carry the idea that we are indispensable in our projects, but we suspect that they could manage without us. Give us rest.

We carry the scars of failure which warn us not to risk ourselves. Give us rest.

We unnecessarily burden ourselves with too much work, too much worry, and too much struggle. Give us the grace to take it easy, Lord.

Let us be lazy every now and then.

Give us rest from our frantic world and burden us with Your world where time is eternal, where guilt is ended, where our wounds are healed, and where we are at rest even as we carry Your burden of love for others.

WE GOT OVER-EXTENDED, LORD

Lord,

We want to be grateful for what we have done and what has been done to us.

We sometimes discover that long ago, past remembering, we got committed to certain people, our parents, our children, our spouses, our jobs, our communities, and friends.

We wake up some days, greatly indebted, over extended and under inspired by our lot.

The grass looks greener in other fields, and our souls, if not our habits, go wandering like lost sheep.

Our eyes go blind to the joys around us, and our tongues go dumb to speaking the needed word.

Lord, send thy miracle working spirits to tend our wandering souls,

    to give back our sight,
    to see the magic empires in our own homes and friends,
    to see the beauty of the people around us,
    and to see the delights of our environments.

And give us back our speech to speak the zestful word of love to the discouraged,

    to speak the corrective word of wisdom to the arrogant,
    to speak the protective word of justice to the harassed
    and helpless.

Lord, we need another miracle, quite a few of them, to make us see and to make us speak Your word of love.

FROM THE PIGPEN, LORD

O Father of our true homeland,

we are prodigals in a far country,

but we would like to arise and come home.

We want to come home from the far country of useless grief

of wasted worries,

of lonely self-interest,

of tired grousing,

of caring what people will think of us,

of unbreakable habits of blind loyalty to wrong things.

We want to come home for surely it is better than competing
with the pigs.

We can now see from the far country that we are homesick,

for home is where grief is under control.

Home is where we only worry about some things not ourselves,

where there is plenty of other interest,

where we are ever refreshed for more impossible human acts,

where we care what the "little" people think,

where habits and customs are roads instead of ruts,

where we are patriots of love and peace and human dignity.

Lord, we are leaving the far country for the near country.

Lord, we are heading home now.

Receive us.

REORDERING PRIORITIES

Lord,

We need some help adjusting our priorities.

The unimportant things keep crowding and shouting their way up to the front of the line.

Our pride, comfort, respectability, esteem, like kids at a ball game, keep hollering "first up"; and humility, sacrifice, concern, and compassion keep ending up in right-field or on the bench.

Lord, help us not to waste our time on the little things or worry over the trivial.

May we set our sights on the big and glamorous things like starving children, dying old people, urban decay, and welfare cases.

Lord, may we praise and follow great heroic people like the smiling nurse, the frolicking child, the dependable plumber or the rabbi carpenter.

And temper our ambitions with the wisdom of the dead whom we all will join in a few years or weeks, so that each day will be a priority day, a celebration day, a Christmas day with lots of bright mysterious packages for people to greet and wonder about; and if they seem so disposed, may we ask them to dance.

LORD OF THE BURNING BUSH

O Thou who hides even Thy name from us because we will use it vainly, but who speaks to us daily in burning bushes, burning cities, burning passions, and enslaved people,

We want ourselves to turn aside and listen to Your call for us, like Moses, to set slaves free.

We so often turn aside to hear You speak of those in the slavery, of sickness, loneliness, and desperation.

We often turn aside and hear You speak of those people bound in the slavery of hunger, war, oppression, illiteracy, and racism.

We often turn aside and hear You speak of those bound in the slavery of their past mistakes, those who sold themselves short, those who expect too much of themselves.

We want ourselves to be free of gods with names who are at our disposal to be kept in our religious box and gods who are only the ghosts of our fears.

Sometimes we listen to You and remember that our days are like grass that grows up and is cut down.

Sometimes we listen to You and remember that as sure as we brought nothing into the world, we can take nothing out of it.

Sometimes we listen to You and remember that our days to love our neighbors to the limit are slipping by.

So, we want ourselves to get organized and get busy freeing all the slaves; but then, who are we to go before the pharaohs who tyrannize us with our busy schedules, guilt, and fear of being embarrassed? Are we afraid of being a fool?

Who are we to run for office, to organize a committee, to teach a class, to learn more, or to take another's job?

Who are we to make a speech, take a petition around, write a letter to the editor or to a politician?

Who are we to overcome our guilt, to correct our mistakes, to really do what we are capable of doing?

Who are we to lead people out of slavery but simple people running and hiding from false authorities whose names we know but fear to speak and reject?

O God, whatever Your name is, whoever You are, we want to be different, we want to be free to be all we are and to do all we can do.

O Thou who is, before Thee we learn who we are—we are those who are <u>ready.</u>

To worship God is to realize that a worm becomes a mighty butterfly without a single command from the Philistine armies.

GOD OF THE REVOLUTION

Lord, take us to Bethlehem where a stable is a palace,
a feeding trough is a throne,
and for a moment nothing is usual.
Lord, take us to Bethlehem where a peasant girl is queen,
a helpless baby is king and the man
of the house only watches by.
Lord, take us to Bethlehem where weakness rules,
the vulnerable are the strong and mere
innocence sends Herod into rage.
Lord, take us to Bethlehem where beaten souls begin to soar,
the humiliated are honored, and the poor are given every benefit.
Lord, take us to Bethlehem where force is mocked by love,
the brutal are tamed and strength is found in failure.
Lord, take us to Bethlehem where our senses,
trained to defenses of long-healed scars,
may feel again the texture of a lively life.
Lord, take us to Bethlehem where our reactions,
trained to fight all enemies of our dead souls,
may respond anew to each would-be friend of our
renewing spirits.
Lord, take us to Bethlehem where our ambitions trained
for suspicion, awaiting ordinary opportunities, may bear such
ambitions lightly expecting rather the unusual in everything.
Lord, take us to Bethlehem where we may be reborn to
a fresh childhood of worldly delights—where our
days are bright with wonder and our souls full to breaking with
wide-eyed anticipation.
Lord, take us to where You are already born and now eagerly await
our coming.

THANKSGIVING

O Giver of Gladness,

We are blessed with riches beyond belief although we find it easy to believe they belong to us.

We have been given too much and we are spoiled into forgetting that the sun does not <u>have</u> to come up, the flowers do not <u>need</u> to bloom, the egg could <u>not</u> hatch and our milk <u>could</u> be sour even if it isn't.

O God of Gladness, surprise us with the little lights so we can be ready for gods of the night who frighten us into thinking we can pray the dawn awake, who frighten us into taking the mystery of growth for our own fertility -- the wonder of fruit for our great productivity - Your possibilities as our necessities.

Save us from the gods who mistake Your gladness for our goodness.

It is good to have the riches we have, but we are glad that riches given us for no good reason at all, make us have choices which the poor can only wish for. We have been given too much.

We will give some of it away.

We are glad for our national prosperity, but overwhelmed by the desire and the need to share it with other people.

We have been given too much; we will let others in on our blessings.

We are glad for this time You have given us. It is good that we have this time. It would be good to have any time, of course, but that does not take from the fact that this time is good.

We are glad we have the place we have. It is good that we occupy this place. It would be good to be in other places, of course, but that does not take away from the fact that this place is good. We have been given too much good land, but we left the bad lands for the First Nations.

We are glad to be born into the families we were born into. It is good that we have had the mothers, fathers, brothers, and sisters we have. Other families are no less because ours is so affirmed by us, of course; but nevertheless, our families are the best ones to have, which is more than enough and too much more than we deserve. Yet we will care for them.

We are glad to have the husbands, wives, and children we have because it is good to form and to be formed by them. You have taken some of them away and we miss them very much. Yet they were too good for our deserving in the first place. We were given too much when we were given the dear ones we were given, but we will care for the loving form they give to our lives as our pain gives way to the care you give to the dead.

Lord, we give thanks for thanksgiving.

Your givings are too much for us to keep to ourselves.

GET US OUT OF THE WAY

Lord,

Take us out of Your way and give us back to Your world.

Make us a means to Your ends.

Remove our timid self-possession so we may be obsessed with Your bold meekness.

May we seek less to teach others and more to learn from them.

May we try less to be correct and more be concerned.

May we strive less to earn our merits and more to find them in others.

May we be satisfied more with another's triumph than with our own success.

May we each day be Your tools for the rebuilding of tenderness into the world, that when we return to the mystery from which we came, let it be that our lives were used by You in life so much that meeting You again will be no surprise to us in death.

AN UPDATED COMMUNION SERVICE

Invitation:

This is a meal for us to share.

This is the table around which we all symbolically sit —hungry for the love Jesus was strong enough to give, thirsty for the courage Jesus was humble enough to have.

Institution:

One night He took bread and tore it up--just the way He was going to be torn up.

He said as He was doing this that the bread represented all that His body already had and was to endure. And He also picked up a cup of wine and held it as if it was the blood that soon would begin to flow out of Him. He said as He was doing this that the vine represented all that He lived for — to write a new law of love on the souls of people. "Eat this my body and drink this my blood as often as you decide to live as I have and endure what I will."

After they killed Him, it finally dawned on the disciples that this kind of a life and death was not only alive in their very bones but that this kind of life and death was the only way to really be alive.

My dear friends who also believe that this is true, this joyful feast is now ready for you to partake. Men and women will come from everywhere, from the Eastern nations and religions we call our enemies and from the Western world, and they will also decide to live undead lives.

What a very great thing it is when we can all live together without fighting. Jesus knew such peace. He offers that peace to you.

Now let us say grace before we eat this great meal.

Blessing:

God is great, God is good, let us thank Him for this food.

Amen.

Holy, holy, holy, Lord God of Hosts. Heaven and Earth are full of Thy Glory.

Glory be to Thee, 0 Lord Most High.

We are now ready to become like Jesus.

This is His body.

[serve]

This is the blood that came from Jesus when religious people and the government executed Him.

[serve]

Ascription of Praise:

Beautiful work, Jesus, that's what we like to see. We never cease to be amazed at the way You can straighten us out even when we are fighting You all the time. Bless You, bless You, bless You! We honor all that You stand for. We glorify the things You did. More power to You.

CHARGE TO CONFIRMANDS

Now you have chosen to be a part of God's people. This does not mean that now you have special claims on God. It means He has special demands for you.

Now you have become a part of the community of saints. This does not mean that you are now a saint. It means that you permit your actions to be judged by theirs.

Now that you have become a self-proclaimed Christian, this does not mean that Christ is at your beck and call. It means that you are available to His leadership.

You now join into full membership of this church. This does not mean that this is the only church or that you now retire to being a club member served by hired ministers. It means that you put yourself willingly within its disciplines and that you now are mobilized into being ministers yourselves who serve humankind, especially those in greatest need.

You now promise to strive to understand God's Word. This does not mean that you simply keep your eyes open during Sunday worship. It means that you commit yourself to serious and regular study of the Bible for its good news.

You agree to participate in the church's activities, worship, and its peace, enlightenment and effectiveness. This does not mean that you will simply send in your weekly tips for a good cause. This means that you find out what its purpose is and that you will encourage, promote and change its activities and worship (where necessary) to be further in line with that purpose.

You say you will try to live a holy and blameless life. This does not mean that you will try to be respectable and proper and moralistic. It means you will be passionately sensitive to the protection of the weak and destitute and that you will be fearless and tireless in the fight against unjust people and systems which cause destitution.

Finally, you agree to further God's Kingdom. This does not mean that you will promote aggressive aspirations of your nation, your business, and your community. But it does mean you will see love, peace, and justice, even in conflict with our government wherever you are and whenever you can—indeed you will seek to go wherever and to be ready whenever this rule of God needs most to be secured.

May God bless you and help you in your costly discipleship.

EPILOGUE

MY CONGRESSIONAL TESTIMONY

The Congressmen seemed moved by my testimony.

Empowerment is words. Certain words at certain places. One place that words can mean empowerment is a Congressional hearing set up to gather facts and views prior to the enactment of legislation. The legislation being enacted when I appeared before a committee of the U. S. House of Representatives was, of all things, the Federal Budget.

As I sat down to the microphone facing the then Congressman from Washington State and Chair of the House Budget Committee,

Brock Adams, I had a dizzy feeling that I gotten myself into the most absurd predicament imaginable. The room was like an old court room with a tall ceiling, wood paneling, and a large raised platform on which twenty or so representatives were to sit staring down at me as I slowly, painfully made a complete fool of myself. "How did I get into this?", I asked myself. "I can't even get my own checkbook to balance, and here I am trying to tell the U. S. Government how to spend billions of dollars. This how it happened.

I came early to the hearing to avoid possible foul-ups mistakes, and misunderstanding that often happens when 5% of my soul tells me to do something crazy like giving congressional testimony; but the other 95% of me wants with all of its wanting power to get out of here and hide in a dark, small cave somewhere very close to my mother who should never have let me out to begin with.

I came so early to that hearing room that no one was in the Rayburn House Office Building except a few security guards getting ready for the day. I know a few of the tricks that the child in me will do to the 5% responsible parent in me who gets me into these terrible predicaments where I find myself presuming to be an expert on things I really find terribly confusing, like the Federal budget. My child will lose things, forget the most important facts or figures or even hide the second page of my great paper from which I am reading my witness. It will give me indigestion or a headache, grave self-doubts, depression or an off-the-wall giggling high—anything to get me out of acting like a responsible citizen, an articulate spokesperson for justice and peace. That is, there is a child in me who uses passive aggression to disempower me, keep me powerless, a docile slave to the fleshpots of comfort and complicity in injustice. It is very tempting to live in powerlessness. Like a child you don't have to be responsible. So, I try to compensate for the tricks by over preparing and double checking out my speech and arriving early.

Slowly the building woke up as I wandered around to find the hearing room. When I found it, it was locked but the number matched the one I had been given by Ruben McCornack, who staffed the Coalition on the National Priorities and Military Policy. My own job in the United Church of Christ (UCC) was to work for peace and new national priorities from the church's perspective. We were a part of the Coalition. This meant trying to empower the churches to use their moral voice to stop the madness in Vietnam, cool down the Cold War, and seek conversion of national resources wasted on the military to fight poverty and other injustices.

It was a great cause. All of it was theologically justified, I thought, after years of academic analysis. But now my job was not academics, but action and challenging power. Not only did I have to try to empower the churches, but I myself had to do what I called on them to do—speak out wherever you can to make a difference—and this was one of those important places in that hearing room #1225 on this day at 10:00 a.m. before the U.S. House Budget Committee.

All educators know that the best learning takes place in action or "learning by doing", as Dewey called it, a concept later rediscovered by Paulo Friere and renamed "consciousization". But there are dangers in doing and action/reflection. For example, you can't put a five-year-old in the driver's seat of a car and tell him to drive. Learning must be managed in sizeable chunks. The great gift we educators give the world is management of the sizeable chunks of learning at teachable moments. How much is appropriate and when?

I was pushing my limits too much by agreeing to analyze the federal budget from a moral perspective, write a paper, and deliver it to Congress. But, as an educator, I know that one of the best ways to educate, that is, manage sizeable chunks of learning for empowering the church was <u>modeling</u>. I had to experience this myself if I would call others to do it. It is just such an act for which Bonhoeffer is listened to as much or more than Barth even though his written works are only a tiny fraction of Barth's. Bonhoeffer <u>did</u> it and died for it. So, we listen to him. He is a model.

I felt I was going to die for it too as I stood alone in the marble corridor waiting for the hearing room doors to open. I found a corner and went over my ten-page paper. It was still too long. But I had cut it down by a half. One of my points was that the President's budget was massively distorted to appear that the military was having to beg for handouts when the opposite was true. But even if you show the numbers, you have to give them flesh and blood on the one hand, tell what this means to hungry children, and, on the other, to do it without getting too emotional.

By 9:30 that morning, I had probably squeezed a week's worth of work into only three months of frantic research. I thought that if I could only get through this agony without fainting or stumbling all over my tongue, then I would have tried to make a difference and have witnessed before Caesar that God is watching our idolatrous amassing of vain chariots. At least I could breathe again and take nourishment. I could, in short, survive my first goal and then tell others with some legitimacy to stand up to the military madness (my second goal).

I had an image of the hearing room scene. There were hundreds of people in a kind of courtroom, 30 or 40 congress people, each with a fawning entourage of assistants, a bank of TV cameras, a scene like say, Watergate Iran Contra hearings. But I had no lawyers on my side, as Oliver North had to snarl like junkyard dogs at lawmakers' questions. The lawyers were on the other side. They were also the lawmakers. By 9:40 my editorial effort had been replaced by my prayer life which was by now getting into high gear. Then Ruben walked up. I hated him. He had gotten me into this. But he was happy, laid back, and jovial. I hated him even more. He did not have to stand before this tribunal and make a fool of himself. But also I loved him, finally a friendly face and support for the ordeal.

He told me who else was giving testimony: someone from SANE, from the Conference of Mayors, and from some unions. I was not exactly going to be the center of attention. I was the liberal church voice as distinct from what most congress people expected of the church—people who especially plead for prayer in schools and tax favors and other sectarian privileges for the church itself. Rather, I was speaking for other causes like peace and justice.

Well, I could be surrounded by other people at the witness table even if I was not center stage. Other learnings followed that and gave me more valuable lessons in humility. None of the television crews had made it yet. I could not catch a glimpse of Tom Brokaw or Peter Jennings. I would have settled for Bill Moyers. There wasn't even any press from our own church's Office of Communications.

The doors opened and I took a deep breath, held Reuben's arm and bravely walked into the room. It was empty. Gradually the other witnesses arrived at about 10 o'clock. I had met them in coalition meetings. But we were hardly close friends. Cold handshakes were barely managed because this was, after all, old hat for them. They gave testimony as if it was calling for room service. They carried only a few notes at most, which they probably had scribbled in the elevator coming up. That made my two 75 lb. briefcases seem out of place. (Just the summary of the Federal Budget weighs five pounds.)

Where were all of the lawmakers eager to hear my brilliant words? Where were the crowds of curious Beltway Bandits, hangers-on, and peace activists? Where was the big brass of the Pentagon, the military contractors, the lobbyists for the Military Industrial Complex and the corporate lawyers to hear me shred their arguments, challenge their livelihoods, and wipe out the merchants of death? Didn't they want to hear what I, their arch enemy, had in store for them? Why weren't they worried enough to be here? Why were there only four of us in a room that could host thousands at this great showdown battle of good and evil?

Eventually an aide to the chair of the House Budget Committee walked in like a bored janitor, placed Brock Adam's nameplate down and rushed off to find something important to do.

Then Adams arrived carrying some papers, smiled and got down to business without waiting for the rest of Congress to show up. He welcomed us and was quite personable. He even seemed somewhat interested for a while, although I began to realize that I was one of very many witnesses he had to sit before in other hearings.

I sat in the middle of the others and drew a middle kind of place in the order. Then my turn came. Would I be able to do it without messing up? I realized that the overly empty room and my come-down from my imaginary image of a hearing turned out to help me psychologically. Presenting my testimony would be more like singing in the shower than preaching in a Roman Colosseum.

Just as I began, another congressman entered and sat down in a kind of slouch. He had no notes and seemed very casual. He was Congressman Parren Mitchell from Baltimore, another relatively liberal voice like Brook Adams, who had long cried in the wilderness on the hill.

I had hardly finished my devastating list of arguments against the military budget when Mitchell sat up. He seemed to actually listen as Adams mumbled to his aide and the other witnesses dozed off, along with the security guards. He leaned forward as I finished and picked right up after my last line. Speaking to me, he said, "I am sorry that more members of the Budget Committee were not here to hear your testimony. . . . For the first time in hearings this year, we have finally touched the whole business of a moral ethic in terms of priority setting in this country. . . . I for one get tired sitting here every day hearing people moan about the deficit. . . with no mention being made at all about morality that ought to exist in this country. . . . Somewhere down the line we have lost our total perspective on this."

Adams stopped whispering to his aide and listened to Mitchell. He smiled and said "Thank you. I particularly appreciate the analysis which you have obviously done in considerable detail." He thanked us all. It would become part of the congressional record. Suddenly it was over. I had survived, my goal one. I did not want to get too elated, however, because I knew that a few words in the congressional record is like a tent in a hurricane. But goal two was accomplished as well. I had done what I taught others to do and had lived to tell about it. I only wished that the church could get more empowered to speak a moral word to Congress so that it would not appear so odd. I took Reuben to lunch. I did not hate him anymore.

LITTLE WOMAN/BIG HEART: LEONA ROSS

Leona did not look like a hard driving social activist.

Once when I was to meet with the Michigan Conference Peace with Justice Committee, the conference staff said that a lay person named Leona Ross would pick me up. Lee did meet me at the Detroit airport and we got into her car for her to drive me to East Lansing. She was very small, almost frail with grey hair and thick glasses. When she started driving, I did not relax. She began telling about a wreck she had just last week. She barely survived but her car was totaled. She said she did not see too well. I did not know her and began to wonder what I was in for. I imagined that one way to punish national staff people if you can't make them move out of New York is to design a disaster to happen and invite us in for it. That ruins our whole day.

This did not slow her down though. (I was wondering if the speed in Michigan was 85 mph!) I was able to see more than she could as she peered through the steering wheel toward the sky. I could see all the dead animals on the road and pot holes and things she was able to hit.

Finally, in spite of it all, we made it to the conference office. I wanted to kiss the ground. The Peace and Justice Committee was waiting for me to speak. After we ate sloppy joes, I did my speech. Then I asked them to tell me what they were doing in their churches for peace and justice.

I had revived from the tension of the ride, but then as I listened I got more and more depressed. There were about 20 people on the committee, and the first 19 of them had the most depressing tales of woe I had ever heard, e.g.,

No one will come out to hear our speakers.

We can't get anyone interested in peace.

All they want is more, not less, military spending.

We tried to have a study of the Just Peace Church, and no one showed up.

We wrote our congressman and he sent back a form letter addressed to "communist occupants."

Our pastor believes we should bomb Moscow, and on and on.

Then finally number 20, Lee Ross, lifted herself up to the
table and said:

"I don't know why you people are so discouraged. At our church,
Salem UCC, we are studying the Just Peace Church book the
second time.

We announce social issues every Sunday in Moments for Mission.

We write letters to congress once a month.

I made 400 peace cranes and took them to Leningrad with a group
and made many Russian friends. I took pictures of them at the war
memorial—a father and his son who splashed in the pot hole water
until his father picked him up. It shows they are real people like us.

I show my slides all over the state now at church groups.

"We're about to turn our congressman around on Contra aid and he's
voted for the South Africa sanctions, thanks to us."

Wow, Lee made my day!

CPSIA information can be obtained
at www.ICGtesting.com
Printed in the USA
BVHW062011140521
607271BV00007B/638